One-on-One

by Marilyn Chassman

Working with Low-Functioning Children with Autism and Other Developmental Disabilities

Author: **Marilyn Chassman**
Editor: **Tom Kinney**
Graphic Design: **Beverly A. Potts**

ISBN: 1-57861-080-X

An IEP Resources Publication

P.O. Box 930250
Verona, WI 53593-0250
Phone: 800-651-0954
Fax: 608-845-8040

Copyright@ 1999, IEP Resources. All Rights Reserved.

Acknowledgements

... all those who have worked with children with autism and have come up with so many good ideas and so many excellent programs

... my family, for their support while I spent so much time working on this book

... our relatives and friends, for their support and for their many gifts of educational supplies for Brian

... our school district, for providing educational software and for providing a communication device for Brian

... all of the dedicated teachers, therapists and consultants who have worked with Brian over the years

... all those who have been praying for Brian, and I wish to thank God for His help

One-on-One

Table of Contents

A Brief Biography of Brian 1
Introduction 5
A Selection of Recommended Curricula 8

PART ONE *Getting Started*

Chapter One	*Beginning to Work with an Aggressive, Low-Functioning Child*	13
Chapter Two	*Starting Out*	19
Chapter Three	*Expanding the Program*	21
Chapter Four	*Record Keeping*	25

PART TWO *Some Specific Therapy Ideas*

Introduction	*Therapy Ideas Section*	41
Chapter Five	*Matching Skills*	
	Breaking Down Picture and Color Matching	43
	Complex Picture Matching	53
	Object to Photo (Picture) Matching	53
Chapter Six	*Receptive Skills*	59
Chapter Seven	*Communication Skills*	
	Beginning to use a Photo Communication System	69
	Using a Communication Device	76
	Using Categories on a Communication Board/Devices	77
Chapter Eight	*Academic Skills*	
	Reading Ideas	83
	Beginning to Type Independently	83
Chapter Nine	*Fine Motor Skills*	
	Writing Ideas	89
	Small Model Work	94
Chapter Ten	*Large Motor Skills: Age-Appropriate Large Motor Work for Self-Esteem*	99
Chapter Eleven	*Computer Skills: Beginning to Use a Computer*	101
Chapter Twelve	*Sensory Work: Sensory Toleration*	103
Chapter Thirteen	*Self-Help Skills: Low Impact Toilet Training*	107
Chapter Fourteen	*Controlling Negative Behaviors: Minimizing Aggression*	111

Summary 115
References 116

One-on-One

A Brief Biography of Brian

There are few children more challenging to raise or teach than those with autism, especially when they're low-functioning. Brian Chassman, the subject of this book, is just such a youth.

That's not to imply that the diagnosis of autism was clear from the beginning. Far from it. As is often the case with children with autism, the specifics of Brian's condition weren't immediately apparent, despite subtle (and not so subtle) indications from the start that things weren't as they should be.

One early sign was his inability to support his head when his parents picked him up. While that's not unusual, it can be an indicator of problems. At six months he had his first neurological exam and was diagnosed with benign hypotonia, defined simply as low muscle tone. It was by definition, benign. Everything still seemed to be okay.

Throughout most of Brian's first two years, despite constant hints of more serious problems, and a slow-burning anxiety on the part of his parents that something was very wrong, they still felt everything would work out in the end.

However, from early on, his mother Marilyn was aware of certain behaviors that were of increasing concern. When she spent time with her friends and their babies, a curious lack of connectedness between Brian and herself was evident. Whereas the other children would move comfortably in and out of their parent's orbit, and show apprehension when a parent left the room, Brian paid little attention to people at all. That included his mother, whose coming and going seemed to be inconsequential to him. This lack of curiosity was not limited to family members. Brian was not much interested in people in general.

In addition, he lagged behind in all areas of motor skill development. He didn't sit up until he was one, nor crawl until 15 months. Language development was pretty near nonexistent.

By the time Brian was two, it was becoming clear that he had significant disabilities. Which disabilities he had, however, were less clear. At that time, doctors were reluctant to give a diagnosis of autism unless it was blatantly obvious. In Brian's case it was anything but.

Nonetheless, the foggy diagnosis of developmental delay was eventually handed down and it was enough to get him enrolled in a preschool special education program. Whatever his problems were, the Chassmans thought they were finally on their way. Now they would get some help.

But in two years of early intervention schooling, Brian was unable to acquire any skills at all. It was, Marilyn says, "very disheartening."

"Everyone was learning except for Brian. You saw all these other kids learning how to sign, learning how to do this, how to do that. They could scribble with crayons, play with Play-Doh and match colors. And these were kids who also had

Brian on top of mountain after a short hike. Age 6.

> *"Because he had motor delays, he was called mentally retarded,"* Marilyn recalls. *"Autism would have been a better diagnosis."*

Biography

One-on-One

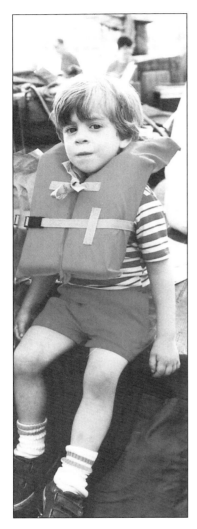

Brian on a boat ride on his fifth birthday.

significant handicaps. But Brian couldn't learn anything."

And he still didn't have an accurate label, something that might have made a significant difference in his early development.

"Because he had motor delays, he was called mentally retarded," Marilyn recalls. "Autism would have been a better diagnosis. Kids who are labeled mentally retarded do try to look at their parents and they try to imitate. They're just slower. Brian's problems were more severe."

Unfortunately, there were no resources in their area for young children with autism, and while they had yet to confirm the diagnosis they felt was inevitable, all signs were pointing in that direction. So, after two years, the Chassmans pulled Brian from early intervention classes and attempted home schooling.

And they took the initiative to look into several of the many highly touted therapies for autism. During the two years Brian was at home, they tried five different approaches. Two were developmentally oriented: The Son-Rise Program and Movement Therapy. The results, Marilyn admits, weren't impressive. "Although Brian did very nicely with the trained therapists, I'm afraid we didn't do either of these therapies properly at home. I'm not very good at doing developmental therapies and I still have a lot to learn."

They also tried Facilitated Communication, and although Brian made little headway with FC, it taught them a valuable lesson—that Brian responded well when people spoke to him as if he was intelligent.

Finally, they did Auditory Training and experimented with Craniosacral Therapy for a year. As a result of all these efforts, there was a marked increase in Brian's sociability. His eye contact improved and for the first time he recognized his parents.

But, despite being more sociable, Brian remained unable to learn any real skills. Looking back, Marilyn realizes that Applied Behavior Analysis (ABA) wasn't widespread at the time and it certainly wasn't an available option in her area. Later she would discover it to be a key ingredient in her self-constructed skills-teaching program for Brian.

The second year at home, Brian (age 5) also attended a regular preschool two days a week. Things went okay there, meaning that while he didn't participate in activities, at least he didn't misbehave horribly. But that was probably because they left him alone and held out few if any expectations for him. Because his behavior was acceptable in that setting, he was next admitted into an inclusive public school classroom.

This placement was to prove a nightmare. Here they did have expectations for Brian and as they attempted to achieve compliance, he acted out. The more they tried to control him, the more contentious he became. He was, Marilyn says simply, "wildly aggressive."

A realist, Marilyn doesn't attempt to downplay Brian's offending behaviors, which she knows better than anyone. "He scratched, grabbed and pinched staff pretty much all day long," she recalls resignedly.

When the year was up, the Chassmans were told Brian was not welcome to return.

At the end of that school year, Brian was re-evaluated and finally received a long overdue diagnosis of autistic spectrum disorder. He was seven.

Brian's next stop was a private school specializing in autism. It was located out of county, which meant he had to undergo an hour-plus school bus ride each way every day. The staff was competent, caring and hard-working...and their effort was all for naught.

"The teachers were wonderful and up-to-date with the latest techniques," Marilyn remembers. "They even tried out my many suggestions, but nothing really worked. Brian continued to be very aggressive and a non-learner."

During Brian's second and last year at the private school, Marilyn resumed her home schooling program in earnest. Two hours a day, every day, the minute he returned from school. This time, however, her ideas and hard work started to take hold.

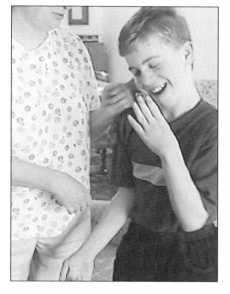

"Brian is now such a happy kid and he is learning. He has many skills and he can reliably communicate his needs and wants."

"The way it happened—with his slow progress—maybe it was better. It's given me the time to think about everything that has worked and to write it down to share with others. And after all, there's so little written material that's helpful for working with low-functioning kids."

Since Brian was finally starting to learn skills for the first time, Marilyn decided to expand the homeschooling program to full days. With constant adjustments and enhancements, Brian's home instruction has continued to the present and constitutes the basis for this manual.

It's been a long haul, but the Chassmans have stayed the course. Once a year they make an extensive home movie of Brian's gains, documenting his slow but inexorable progression forward. As one watches these productions, one thing is achingly clear: working with an aggressive, low-functioning child with autism requires a level of patience, perseverance and ingenuity few possess.

One-on-One

And, in turn, this manual asks a lot from the dedicated instructor—parent or teacher—who's undertaking the mission of working with a child like Brian. But it asks no more than the Chassmans have asked of themselves over the years: hard work (often with negligible progress), one-on-one instruction and an eclectic approach that combines bits and pieces of many methods.

The bottom line is that the work is worth it. According to Marilyn, "Brian is now such a happy kid and he is learning. He has many skills and he can reliably communicate his needs and wants."

And since writing this book, Marilyn has been in contact with some leading experts in the field of autism, many of whom have been impressed with her work. In fact, Dr. Bernard Rimland, director of the Autism Research Institute, recommended she send this manual—originally self-published—to IEP Resources. This manual, Dr. Rimland comments, "...will be of great value to parents and teachers of low-functioning autistic children."

And Dr. Gary Mesibov, director of the University of North Carolina's TEACCH initiative—a groundbreaking program for working with children with autism—paid Marilyn the highest compliment, noting "...several members of our program have found a number of your ideas and ways of working with your youngster to be extremely useful for the children and families we work with.

"Thank you for your important contributions to our efforts."

For a parent with no professional background in education (Marilyn's a computer programmer), who's self-taught, this experience hasn't just been an intense labor of love—it's been quite an accomplishment.

Mar. 24, 1999

Tom Kinney, Editor

Introduction

This book contains the ideas that allowed my son Brian to learn a number of new skills. I have written it in the hope that it will help others. While Brian is still far from being cured, he has progressed from having no skills and many bad behaviors to learning at an increasing rate and being relatively well-behaved. Since many older, low-functioning autistic children tend to progress slowly or not at all, I believe the ideas that have helped him may be of significance. Also, because of the common sense nature and behavioral-oriented approaches followed here, I believe they may be useful for helping low-functioning children with diagnoses other than autism.

This book presents some new methods for teaching a number of matching skills. It also suggests ideas for teaching a wide range of other topics, from dealing with haircuts to using a computer.

The information presented here isn't intended to be a complete program. Instead, it's designed to give you useful 'pieces' to add to existing comprehensive programs. Ideally, all low-functioning children with autism are already in programs that teach skills systematically. Use the ideas in this book either to supplement those programs, or as alternatives to be tried when children are unable to learn particular skills.

Brian is slowly working through the steps of an excellent comprehensive program, LINKS to Language. In fact, Brian's entire program consists of material from the Links program, as well as from several other methods, plus what is written here. I've blended these approaches together, rather than just staying with one, because this is what's worked best for Brian.

Brian and Mom watching a parade. He's wearing headphones because the drums and fire sirens are too loud.

Brian enjoying himself at the beach. Age 11.

One-on-One

Brian and Mom on a camping trip. Age 11½.

Brian has a lot less going for him than other children diagnosed with autism. At age two, he had moderate to severe delays in fine and gross motor skills, no receptive language, no words, an inability to imitate anything, and an almost total lack of interest in people. He would look at people only if they made an enormous effort: nothing short of jumping up and down and dancing a jig could capture his attention. And he was unaware of people around him. When someone entered or left the room, he took no notice. Yet, when a new toy was placed nearby, he was immediately aware of it.

Since Brian had delays in fine and gross motor skills and because he could be engaged by others at least briefly, doctors shied away from giving him a diagnosis of autism. At the age of two, I was told that Brian was mentally retarded, and he was diagnosed with developmental delay. Ultimately, it was his lack of interest in people and his total inability to imitate that posed the most significant problems. Since Brian never looked at us nor imitated anything we did, there was no chance he would ever be able to learn skills. So an early diagnosis of autism would have been helpful. It would have steered us towards therapies that would help him learn to imitate. However, it wasn't until after Brian became school age that he received an unequivocal diagnosis of autistic spectrum disorder.

Let me digress briefly: there are a number of excellent programs designed to help children with autism. Most begin by teaching them how to imitate simple skills, since this is something they have a hard time with. But low-functioning children with other diagnoses can also have trouble with imitation and often their teachers and parents aren't aware of these programs for children with autism that would be helpful for them. From what I've seen, children with autism in school settings often get more intensive services than those with other diagnoses, yet all kids with severe behavior problems and few skills need intensive therapy. New programs need to be developed to meet their needs and I hope some of the material in this book may serve that purpose.

Although we tried many therapies over the years, by the time Brian was eight, he still had few skills. On one hand, he had become more sociable and happy, but in other ways, things were worse. He was aggressive when confronted with almost any demand and still wasn't toilet trained. His fine motor skills consisted of being able to eat with a spoon, put in a few pieces of an easy inset puzzle, and drop blocks in a bucket. He remained incapable of holding a crayon to do even the most basic scribbling. His large motor skills consisted of being able to walk and climb stairs. Yet he couldn't throw a ball; didn't appear to understand any language; couldn't match objects, pictures, colors, or shapes; wouldn't tolerate haircuts; couldn't sign and wouldn't imitate anything we said or did.

But at eight, I began to have success with Brian using some ideas that eventually grew into the contents of this book. As of this writing, at the age of twelve, he has a number of skills and his behavior is much improved. He's rarely aggressive and is toilet trained. He can match pictures, colors, objects and shapes. He uses over 100 photos for communication purposes and is starting to use a main menu of picture symbols. He has up to twenty photos on his schedule board each day. He runs five programs on a computer independently. He can copy drawing simple shapes and is able to trace many letters. He types words independently if he can see how they're spelled. He puts together pieces from small model kits independently. He rides a bicycle without training wheels. He throws; he hits a ball off a batting tee; he in-line skates. He's good with haircuts, can copy ten gestures and several sounds, and can use a few signs. He's beginning to understand more of what we say.

These advancements of Brian's may seem trivial to parents who have high expectations for their children, but relative to where he was at just a few years ago, to us they are milestone achievements.

While it's important to note that much of this is anecdotal, some of these approaches have already been used successfully with other low-functioning children who were able to gain skills they had previously been unable to acquire. They've worked for us and we've seen them work for others.

Being well acquainted with autism, I don't expect all of the ideas here to work for all children. But some children should benefit from some of these ideas. If controlled studies are ever done on any of the approaches presented here, they may find some of these techniques to be the best first choice for the low-functioning population.

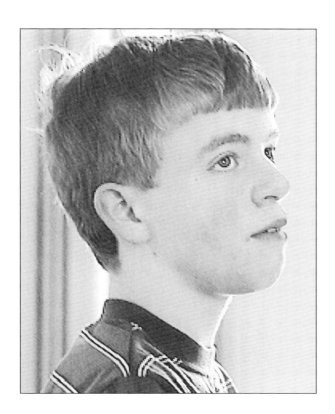

I began to have success with Brian using some ideas that eventually grew into the contents of this book. As of this writing, at the age of twelve, he has a number of skills and his behavior is much improved.

Recommended Curricula

A Selection of Recommended Curricula

I have used the following curricula and instructional materials to varying degrees in my work with Brian and I recommend all of them:

Behavioral Intervention for Young Children with Autism: A Manual for Parents & Professionals, edited by Catherine Maurice, coedited by Gina Green & Stephen C. Luce, 1996, PRO-ED

Teaching Developmentally Disabled Children: The ME Book, by O. Ivar Lovaas, 1981, PRO-ED

Breakthroughs: How To Reach Students With Autism, by Karen Sewell, 1998, Attainment Company, Inc.

PECS Training Manual, by Lori A. Frost and Andrew S. Bondy, 1994 by Pyramid Educational Consultants, Inc.

The Carolina Curriculum for Infants and Toddlers with Special Needs, Second Edition, by Nancy M. Johnson-Martin, Kenneth G. Jens, Susan M. Attermeier and Bonnie J. Hacker, 1991, Paul H. Brooks

The Carolina Curriculum for Preschoolers with Special Needs, by Nancy M. Johnson-Martin, Susan M. Attermeier and Bonnie J. Hacker, 1990, Paul H. Brooks

LINKS to Language is available only through a training session. For information write Help Associates, P.O. Box 43515, Upper Montclair, NJ, 07043. (973-746-5782)

Life skills curricula designed for secondary students and adults with developmental disabilities:

Looking Good (a personal care program) and *Keeping House* (a housekeeping skills program) are available from Attainment Company, Inc.

Curricula

Recommended Curricula

It's a good idea, when attempting to work with low-functioning children, to be knowledgeable about the following approaches: ABA methodology, TEACCH program, *LINKS to Language* and the *Picture Exchange Communication System (PECS)*. When possible, read about, observe and become trained in these techniques. In addition, there are several developmental methods that can greatly enrich your program: *Stanley Greenspan's Floor Time, The Miller Method* and the *Son-Rise Program.*

While TEACCH doesn't publish a curriculum *per se,* it offers training programs for those interested in its techniques. Intensive one-week training programs are held each summer, while less intensive regional programs are available throughout the year. For more information, contact the TEACCH training coordinator at: 919-966-4126. Or you can visit their website at *www.unc.edu/depts/teacch/teacch.htm.*

The PECS Training Manual is authored by Lori A. Frost and Andrew S. Bondy of Pyramid Educational Consultants, Inc. Pyramid has consultants available to help with aspects of their program. You can check their website at *www.pecs.com* or call them at 888-832-7462.

In Brian's case, I've taken ideas from all these programs in pretty much equal doses, since there was no single approach that was highly effective with him. I suspect that's the case with other low-functioning children as well. The more ideas and techniques you're conversant with, the more likely you can adapt an individualized program for your low-functioning student or child.

> *There's never just one way to teach a child.*
>
> — *Marilyn Chassman*

Curricula

PART ONE
Getting Started

"I had no training, nor was I following a formal program. But I read up on it and gave it my best shot."

Chapter One

Beginning to Work with an Aggressive, Low-Functioning Child

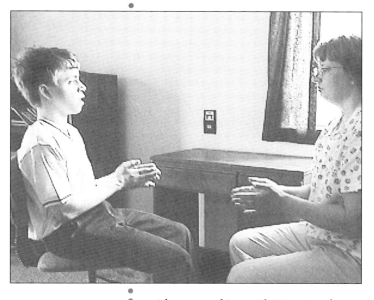

I began working with Brian two hours a day. We worked on the motor imitation skill of clapping his hands.

When Brian was eight, he was extremely aggressive in response to almost all demands. He was even aggressive when called to the table for a meal. When I'd ask him, he'd get upset because it interrupted whatever he was doing at the moment—his routine. In addition, he didn't seem to grasp my request and he didn't like doing something he didn't understand. Of course, once he got to the table and realized it was time to eat, he'd calm down and everything was fine. The problem was getting him from where he was to where he needed to be. He tended to get "stuck" in what he was doing, didn't know how to transition out of it, and emphatically resisted any change of routine. Almost all typical work-related demands were also greeted with aggression: mostly grabbing, pinching and scratching, but sometimes kicking, lunging and attempting to bite.

In addition to aggression, Brian seemed unable to learn any skills, despite our having tried a number of approaches. It was a difficult time. Fortunately, I came across Applied Behavioral Analysis about this time and decided to try some of these ideas with Brian. I'd had no training in this approach, nor was I following a formal ABA program. But I read up on it and gave it my best shot.

I began by working with Brian two hours a day. Given his extremely low level of functioning and his severe aggression, this was as much as I could handle. I started by having him work on the motor imitation skill of clapping his hands once. Although he was eight years old, he couldn't do it. He couldn't do any motor imitation.

I had a variety of reinforcers I used to reward Brian: food, drink, a number of toys, tickling, tossing him in the air, swinging him around, etc. I would model clapping and then help him to clap (right away) when he didn't respond. He would receive a reward each time, even if I had to help him clap.

Beginning to Work with an Aggressive, Low-Functioning Child

On the first day, the work went well. Brian was only aggressive a little bit, and he seemed to enjoy the reinforcers. He even clapped his hands once, unprompted, during the two hours that we worked.

But the next several days didn't go well at all. He was already tired of the reinforcers, and spent most of his time screaming and being aggressive. It was increasingly difficult for me to maintain my enthusiasm. To be honest, I didn't feel like doing fun things with him, like tickling him or swinging him around, because he spent most of his time attacking me.

After four days, I concluded that what I was doing was not going to work.

Fortunately, right at that time, I got an idea for a much better reinforcer from watching a therapist work with a friend's child in an Applied Behavioral Analysis program. When this child finally did a task correctly, he was praised and he got one great, big reward: he was allowed to stop working.

I based my entire program on the reinforcer that if Brian completed a task correctly, he was praised and was allowed to stop working.

I liked this idea a lot. It was something I thought might work with Brian. It was so simple I felt I could do it under extreme stress, such as when he was screaming and being aggressive. I wouldn't have to do any rational thinking like, "Hmm, I just gave him a toy on the last try, maybe this time I should tickle him..." all while being attacked. All the reinforcers, except for praise and knowing he had finished the job, would be unnecessary.

I began again using this new reinforcer. In fact, I based my entire program on it. This time, we worked on the motor imitation skill of patting the knees with both hands. It was still awful. He screamed a lot and was very aggressive, but I held firm. He wasn't allowed to leave his chair until he patted his knees once. In the beginning, this often took the full two hours.

If I had started Brian imitating simple actions using objects, rather than working on motor imitation, it might not have taken him so long to complete a single task once. "Some children learn object-mediated imitation (*e.g.*, ringing a bell, placing a block in a bucket) faster than gross motor movements."[1] At that point, Brian could put blocks in a bucket. Other tasks we might have tried include: pushing a toy car, putting a peg in a pegboard, and a piece in an inset puzzle. We could have built a large repertoire of these imitative actions before starting on the more difficult motor imitation tasks.

For the first few weeks, we worked exclusively on one task, patting his knees, but soon it only took him an hour to do it one time. So I added a task for the second hour. After two months, he could do seven tasks in two hours. After six months, he was able to go through 50–75 tasks in a two-hour period. This sounds like a lot, but these tasks were often simple: *e.g.*, clapping his hands once counted as a task.

Beginning to Work with an Aggressive, Low-Functioning Child

I stuck to the "once, only" rule without deviation. We never repeated a task during the two-hour work period. All 50–75 tasks were different. When he was done, that was it. That was the rule. The beauty part was that he seemed to understand: if he did what I asked once, he wouldn't have to do it again. Conversely, if he didn't do it, I wouldn't leave him alone. Maybe that's the part he really got!

Working on many skills for short periods was also helpful in mediating his aggression. At this point, there were no tasks that he loved doing. Keeping it short and sweet kept him in a better mood.

I did the same tasks with him everyday. That way, he got a little bit of practice on many skills on a regular basis. The tasks were always done in the same order, giving the program a well-defined structure, and it helped him to know what was coming next. It also made it a lot easier for me. I didn't have to think, "Now, what should we do next?" I already knew. Remember, Brian was frequently aggressive during the sessions; the less creative thinking I needed to do while working, the better.

He did almost all work at his desk. When he was done with a task, Brian was allowed to get down from the chair and play with toys for about a minute. Then he had to come back for the next task. When he didn't come back willingly, I would pick him up and carry him. Within a few weeks he came back almost every time.

When he was up to doing multiple tasks, I would group 5–7 of them into a work segment. Each segment would last 10–15 minutes. As mentioned, Brian would get a brief break after each completion. After an entire segment was finished, he would get a five minute break while I put away materials and got out new ones. When all of the work segments were done or the two hours were up, he was done for the day, and got a big reward; a video or a special toy.

It didn't always run smoothly. In the beginning there was a lot of aggression. Quickly, I discovered I didn't always have the stamina to wait him out on every battle. After a bit of thought, I came up with the "15-minute rule":

> *When the child is starting to be successful in a number of areas, be sure to start him working through an established, comprehensive program.*

The 15 Minute Rule

Whenever Brian became uncooperative during a task, I would set a timer for 15 minutes and would continue to work with him throughout that time. If he did what was asked, he was done and I put the timer away. However, if he failed to do it by the time the bell rang, we would stop working on the task and move on to the next one. When it was complete, we would go back to the task he had refused to do, again setting the timer and working on it for 15 minutes, or until he did it successfully. We would continue coming back to the task he didn't complete until he would finally do it.

Sometimes this meant we worked longer than our two-hour period, and occasionally we'd go well into the evening. Once in a while, I had to carry over two or more tasks with the timer. The most I repeated a task was seven times. I made a point of being very consistent. Once Brian figured this out, we didn't have to use the timer very often.

Chapter One 15

Beginning to Work with an Aggressive, Low-Functioning Child

Although he did many activities each day, the focus was not on getting through a certain number of tasks, but on having him do each task well. Half-hearted, sloppy responses weren't acceptable. A precise result was defined and expected for each task. If he took a long time to do a task, that was fine. I would sit and wait and encourage and prompt him until he would do it well, even if it meant that we didn't get through all the activities that day. That was absolutely okay.

And once he was able to do a task independently, he was done with it.

Some tasks were more difficult, however, and I didn't expect him to perform them independently right away. During a work session, we would practice running through each of these tasks once hand-over-hand. In order to be done with a task, Brian had to perform at the highest level of accomplishment he had shown in previous attempts. If he made a lackluster effort, he would have to do it again and again until he did the best he could. Over time, I would try to fade my support.

All tasks, whether done independently or with help, had to be completed without aggression, screaming or crying.

I held out hope that Brian was intelligent. I didn't know what he would be able to learn and I wanted to give him a lot of opportunity.

Even if he performed a task perfectly, if he was behaving poorly, it didn't count and he had to do it again. No amount of aggression would get him out of a task, nor would it make the task easier for him.

These approaches went a long way towards improving his behavior. By the end of the first year, his aggression level was one-fourth of what it had been when we began.

The tasks I chose represented a wide range of skill levels. I held out hope that Brian was intelligent, and since he was older, I wanted to include age-appropriate tasks in his program. I also incorporated low-level tasks because I believed they were important. I didn't know what he would be able to learn, and I wanted to give him a lot of opportunities. We could always drop tasks that didn't work out, and expand ones that went well. One thing was certain: if we didn't work on a task, it wouldn't get learned.

Chapter One

Beginning to Work with an Aggressive, Low-Functioning Child

I want to add that because I felt Brian might be intelligent, I always spoke to him with age-appropriate language. I did not use truncated sentences. I did this during work and free time.

Over time, it has become apparent that it was a good idea to work on a wide range of skills. Overall, Brian made as much progress on high-level skills as he did on low-level ones. I won't list all the tasks we did that first year, since Brian didn't make equal progress on every skill. Also, I don't want to steer people in the wrong direction. Ultimately, it's best to follow an established curriculum. If I were to start again, I would choose tasks differently than I did. The first year we worked together, I wasn't following the steps of a comprehensive program: however, it would have been to Brian's benefit if I had been. As mentioned before, I probably wouldn't have started with motor imitation skills. These were (and continue to be) fairly difficult for Brian; imitating actions on objects would have been easier for him. Also, I would have included more tasks that were broken down to a very low level so Brian wouldn't have experienced so much frustration.

Does teaching an aggressive child always require a battle of wills? I sure hope not, but I don't know. I suspect you'd have fewer problems if each task could be broken down so far that the child experiences success from the start. One wonderful thing I've noticed is when I finally present Brian with a task truly at his level, he is absolutely happy and pleased to do it. It's always obvious when I get it right. There is such a difference in his demeanor. He is so proud he can do the work.

I've been able to break down a few tasks *(see Part Two, Some Specific Therapy Ideas)* into smaller, digestible pieces for Brian. Hopefully, these will also be helpful for other low-functioning children. Speaking of simplification, the technique I have presented in this chapter for working with Brian is based almost entirely on two approaches: the "once, only" rule and the concept of always presenting tasks in the same order. When the rules became this simple, Brian was finally able to start learning.

> *One wonderful thing I've noticed is when I finally present Brian with a task truly at his level, he is absolutely happy and pleased to do it. It's always obvious when I get it right.*

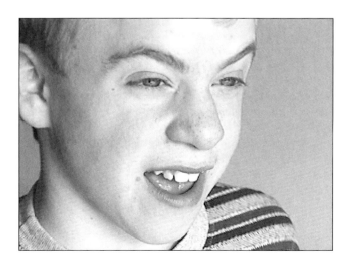

Chapter One 17

Chapter Two

Starting Out

Here are some ideas for beginning a program with a low-functioning child who has few if any skills:

First, have the child learn some simple fine motor skills, like putting pegs in a pegboard, putting pieces in simple inset puzzles, and placing magnets on a magnetic board. Start with just one of these skills and have him put in just one of these pieces, *e.g.*, have him put one peg in a pegboard, and then he is *done* for the day. If this skill is very easy for him, of course, have him do the other two skills also (with a single piece each). However, if putting a single peg into a pegboard proves to be a struggle, then just doing this one skill is enough.

Gradually, have him do all three of these skills (with each skill presented separately), and gradually have him put several pieces in each (always set out all of the pieces at the beginning of the task so that he knows when the task is complete). Other simple fine motor tasks can be chosen in place of these tasks, if for any reason they prove to be too difficult for the child. For example, the task of "putting blocks into a bucket" could substitute for any of the tasks listed above.

> *First, have the child learn some fine motor skills, then introduce picture and color matching.*

Putting pegs in a pegboard is a good example of a simple fine motor task.

Starting Out

After the child can easily perform a few fine motor skills, introduce picture and color matching as described in Chapter Five, *Breaking Down Picture and Color Matching into pieces smaller than you would ever imagine*.

Gradually, add the following pieces to the child's program, in any order:

- Have the child learn to hold a marker and to make a single mark on a wipe-off board, independently. After this, move on to the work described in the Chapter Nine, *Fine Motor Skills (see page 89)*.
- Begin a toilet training program during the evening, as described in Chapter Thirteen, *Self-Help Skills (see page 107)*.
- Set aside a 5–15 minute period to read to the child, and have him learn to sit quietly.
- Introduce some large motor skills, like throwing, catching, rolling, or kicking a ball.
- Start working on computer mouse use, as mentioned in Chapter Eleven, *Beginning to Use a Computer (see page 101)*.
- Start a Sensory Toleration program, as specified in Chapter Twelve, *Sensory Work (see page 103)* and teach the child to tolerate everyday items or events like wearing a hat or getting a haircut.

When the child is starting to be successful in a number of areas, be sure to have him begin to work through an established, comprehensive program.

An example of a large motor skill is playing with a ball.

Chapter Two

Chapter Three

Expanding the Program

Brian made so much progress during the first year of his two hour a day program, by that summer I decided to add to it. His behavior was much better. He almost always cooperated while working and he was actually learning skills. I felt I could handle expanding his program from two hours a day, seven days a week, to five and a half hours a day, five days a week. It worked, and we've continued with this schedule to the present day.

The overall design for Brian's program is always evolving. He no longer does work segments of five to seven unrelated tasks, but now works on twelve different program components. These include:

- Matching
- Receptive Skills
- Communication
- Academic
- Fine Motor
- Large Motor
- Computer
- Self-Help Skills
- Sensory Work

We also work on Vocational, Music and Art Skills, although these aren't mentioned in this book. Much of the work that we cover in all of the various skill areas is from other programs. Not all of the work that we do is included in this book.

Because these components are not equally important, and because we don't have time to do all of them every day, we no longer work on every skill, every day, as we did the first year. I prioritized each component and decided if it should be done four or five days a week. Then I put together a weekly schedule that reflects these choices. Brian's schedule varies day to day.

I use a photo schedule showing each day's tasks to help Brian deal with a changing timetable. We were able to implement the schedule once Brian understood object to photo matching.

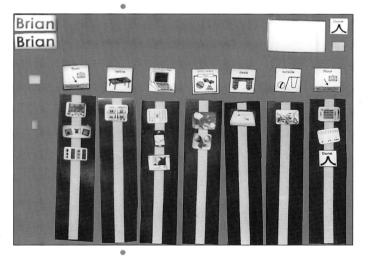

I use photo schedules showing daily tasks to help Brian deal with a changing timetable. The first set of tasks has been completed and removed from the schedule. (This schedule combines ideas from the TEACCH program with some of my own).

Expanding the Program

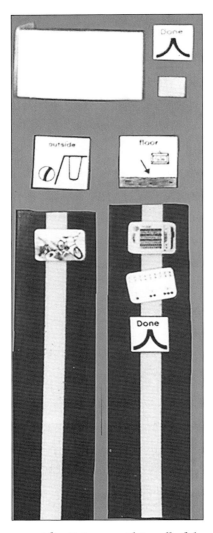

After Brian completes all of the work for the day, he gets a reward, which changes from day to day. (The photo of the reward is hidden under the "done" symbol at top right.) This schedule uses ideas from the TEACCH program.

Moving Past the "Once, Only" Rule

In order to learn skills at a faster rate, it's necessary for Brian to practice some skills more than once a day. To do this without breaking my rule and frustrating him in the process, I found several visual strategies that let him know how many repetitions were expected of him before he began a particular task.

One helpful strategy when doing sorting or assembly tasks was to lay out all the training materials in front of him at the beginning of the exercise. That served to make it clear to Brian that when all the objects, pictures or pieces were "used" he was done with the task.

Another excellent approach was a pegboard strategy from TEACCH (a statewide program in North Carolina). This is a token system, in which a full pegboard marks the end of the task. It worked best with tasks that didn't have a clear ending. An example was our work with receptive labeling, where I would ask Brian to point to one of two objects for a total of ten correct responses. Each time he responded correctly, he received a peg, which he placed in a 10 hole pegboard. When the pegboard was filled, I would help him sign "done" and let him leave.

A third strategy is included in Chapter Nine *Fine Motor Skills (see page 89)*. In it I describe a stencil with three openings for drawing vertical lines. If Brian did the stencil once, he would draw three vertical lines, hence getting in some repetition. It may seem like a subtle distinction, but he was more comfortable doing a three line stencil once, instead of a single line stencil three times.

We still find the "once, only" rule invaluable and continue to use it with many tasks. However, when I want Brian to complete more than one repetition of a task, I always use one of the above strategies so he knows in advance what is expected of him.

Having said this, it should be noted that Brian is now able to work willingly on a few tasks (mostly fine and large motor skills as well as computer games) without these strategies. In fact, he doesn't even need to see the photo on the schedule board. In other words, without any advance warning we can work on these skills during a number of repetitions. When a child is able to work on a skill repetitively without problems, go ahead and do it. There's no need to use these strategies every time. When they're not necessary, they're cumbersome.

Determining the Number of Repetitions of a Given Task

Before we discuss the issue of task repetition, I want to expand on the TEACCH pegboard mentioned in the previous section. Begin by purchasing a pegboard set (available in educational stores), and cut the pegboard into pieces containing the number of holes you need (*e.g.,* 2, 3, 4, 5, 6, 8, 10, 12). In other words, make as many different-sized small pegboards as you can from the original. Use the small pegboards to show the child how many repetitions he's expected to do (see Figure 1).

Expanding the Program

When Brian and I start on a new task that he may find difficult, I use a pegboard with 2 or 3 holes, so he has only to make several correct responses to be done. When he becomes accustomed to the task and it's no longer aversive to him, he still needs to work toward mastery. Then, I gradually move up to 8, 10 and 12 hole pegboards. At this point, he's getting in more work, and is more likely to start learning the skill. But Brian must make good responses to get each peg. He doesn't get a peg simply for completing a trial with an incorrect response; pegs must be earned. I should also note that I usually vary the problem to be solved for each peg; *e.g.,* once he has shown me "book" correctly, I may ask him to show me "ball" on the next trial. I only repeat a trial exactly if he gets it wrong, and then I repeat it until he has gotten it right. *(Note: sometimes I do repeat a trial exactly even if he has responded correctly, just to be truly random when presenting the task.)* Asking Brian to do exactly the same task ten times in a row to earn ten pegs might result in him giving me incorrect answers because he would wonder if his previous responses were wrong; "Why does Mom keep asking me to do this same problem over and over again unless I'm wrong?"

Occasionally, I decide a skill is so important we will work on it all day and neglect others. I may work on a single skill for several days or even weeks, bringing out the 8, 10 or 12 hole pegboards (or the materials to be sorted) many times throughout each day. Brian is not always thrilled about this, but he adjusts to it, and sometimes it's necessary to work intensively to learn a particular skill. We have done this with several skills: color matching, the photo-to-object "give me" task *(see Chapter Seven, Beginning to Use a Photo Communication System, page 69)*, and receptive labeling. Working on one skill for a whole day (or many days) results in an unbalanced program, but occasionally it is necessary for him to leap ahead. However, using the 8, 10 or 12 hole pegboards to get in 8, 10, or 12 good repetitions, or the alternative, sorting through a set of 10–20 items once a day, usually is sufficient for him to learn most skills.

After Brian achieves mastery of a skill—defined as 100% accuracy over a few sessions—I stop formal work on it and move on to something else. I occasionally ask him to perform the skill in review, but I usually only ask for 2 or 3 correct responses. If he does poorly, we will resume formal work on it. But if he's accurate, I assume all is fine. I never ask him to perform a task over and over again just because he is able to do it. This could result in him losing the skill because he would start to think his responses were incorrect. There are thousands of skills low-functioning children need to learn. Working within an established curriculum helps to know what to do next.

Figure 1 Small pegboards can be used to show the child how many repetitions he is expected to do.

Chapter Three

Chapter Four

Record Keeping

y record keeping method is concise and easy to do. I have a shorthand system that works well.

First, I list all tasks Brian will do that day. As he does each one, I note anything new. If we try a new approach or a more difficult level of the skill, it's duly recorded. If Brian makes progress on the task, it's written down. However, if we're doing the task the same as before, there's no need to write about the methodology. And if Brian's work on the task is about the same as it was the day before (*i.e.*, no progress), then I just put a zero next to where the task is written, rather than writing about it in detail.

In addition, to track Brian's behavior, I mark a plus or minus sign next to each task. A plus means he was happy and cooperative during the time we worked on the task. A minus means anything from a little grumbling and whining to full-fledged screaming, while two minus signs means aggression. When there's minus signs, I record what happened and what might have triggered the behavior.

Five to ten minus signs in a row for a given task indicates the need for a change of approach to that skill. Seeing five to ten zeros in a row for a particular task means Brian has plateaued on learning the skill and is making no further progress. It also means I need to change my approach to this task.

Doing record keeping this way saves time but still tracks necessary information.

Recording Skills

• Suggested Skill Areas

At the right margin are the skill areas that I have used for categorizing the skills I do with Brian. They are not in any sort of priority order.

There are many different ways of classifying the skills to be learned. For example, receptive skills and matching skills are sometimes grouped together in a category called Cognitive Skills. I've also seen receptive skills grouped in with communication skills. Self-help skills and vocational skills are sometimes grouped together as Daily Living Skills. Feel free to use whichever skill areas make the most sense for the child and the curriculum.

This chapter contains reproducible record keeping forms and sample forms that have already been filled out.

Suggested Skill Areas

*Communication
Matching
Receptive
Academic
Art
Self-Help
Vocational
Sensory
Music
Social
Computer
Fine Motor
Gross Motor
Behavior*

Record Keeping

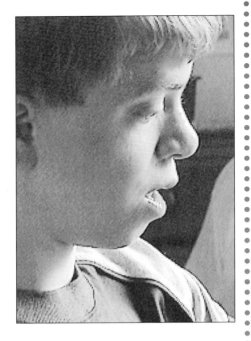

- **Suggested Symbols for Rating Behavior, Performance and Progress**

Below are the symbols that I am currently using to rate Brian's behavior, performance and progress. Note that one can use alternate symbols on any of the forms. There is no key specified on any of the forms (in part, to give the user more space to write comments), and the teacher can use whatever grading system is most appropriate.

For example, a teacher may wish to track the total number of incidents of aggression that occurred while working on a particular skill rather than just tracking whether or not aggression occurred at all. Or, a teacher may wish to track a behavior problem other than aggression that interferes with the child's work. Teachers may wish to specify performance as a numerical ratio, *e.g.,* 7/10, etc. The forms are designed to give the user flexibility with grading.

Suggested Rating Symbols

BEHAVIOR	
+	work is done happily
-	work is NOT done happily *(e.g., some crying or screaming, but no aggression)*
=	some aggression
≡	severe aggression

PERFORMANCE	
N	not grasping concept; less than 60% correct; cannot do any part of the task independently
L	low level performance; starting to grasp concept; 60-75% correct; can do part of the task independently, but still needs help with other parts
H	high level performance; 80-95% correct; nearly independent with task
M	mastered; 100% correct; completely independent

PROGRESS	
FT	first time task was presented
I	some improvement noted
O	performance about the same as last time
↓	performance not as good as last time

Record Keeping

- **Sample Planning Form**

Student Name: Brian				Goals for Year 2000
Skill Area: Matching				

SKILL				INITIAL PROCEDURE/MATERIALS (can indicate one or more alternatives)
match picture symbols to photos (for 8 different photos of objects – 5 different picture symbols per photo)				Make first set of picture symbols by tracing the photos and then coloring in the drawings in a manner similar to the photos. When he can match these drawings to the photos, make more copies of the drawings and either leave them uncolored, or color them differently. See if he can match these to the photos. Gradually have him match different picture representations of the objects to the photos. At first, try with just single pictures (to match to the photos). If this doesn't work, try the multiple photo/multiple picture symbol idea mentioned in the Object to Photo (Picture) Matching chapter of this book.
START	LOW	HIGH	MASTERED	
9/15/00	9/15/00	10/23/00		
match words (up to 5 letters long)				At first have him compare words that look very different, e.g., a 2-letter word vs. a 5-letter word. Gradually have the words look more alike. Try with pairs at first; if this doesn't work, make multiple copies and have him practice stacking these together as in the Picture and Color Matching chapter of this book. Use word cards with large (one-inch) letters.
START	LOW	HIGH	MASTERED	
9/15/00	9/15/00	10/2/00	10/17/00	
match equal quantities (for quantities of 1, 2 and 3)				Start with picture cards that have one, two or three black dots. Have multiple copies of each. When he can match these well, make up new picture cards with one, two or three slightly larger black dots. See if he can match the larger dots to the smaller dots by quantity. Next, try another set of picture cards that are slightly different from the large dots (maybe a slight change of color), etc.
START	LOW	HIGH	MASTERED	
9/15/00	9/22/00	9/29/00		
match objects by size (big/little)				Use multiple identical large plastic items vs. multiple identical small plastic items (no mixed shapes or colors). Gradually try a mixed grouping. Also can try pairs of very large items vs. very small items.
START	LOW	HIGH	MASTERED	
10/18/00				
match objects that belong together (e.g., toothbrush with toothpaste) (4 different pairs)				Use procedure and materials described on page 10 of curriculum ABC. An alternative approach is described on page 42 of curriculum XYZ; this can be tried if the first method doesn't work.
START	LOW	HIGH	MASTERED	

This form lists IEP (or other) goals for the student. It also has spaces for planned procedures and materials to be used and dates when the student starts the work and when he reaches increasing levels of mastery.

There are two innovations (I think) on this form. The first is that instead of just specifying a start date and complete date, I've added two other dates that can be noted: the date when the student reaches a low level of performance on the skill, and the date when the student can do the skill with a high level of performance. Because low-functioning children can be very slow to master a skill, noting that the child has made at least *some* progress can offer encouragement to the teacher. Also, if a child can do four steps independently out of a five-step task, it's nice to be able to write this down, rather than having to wait until every single part of the task is absolutely perfect.

The other innovation on this form is that I've written *Initial Procedure/Materials* rather than *Procedure/Materials*. This wording will hopefully move people away from the mindset that there is only one particular way to teach a skill; that if something isn't working, one *should* try something else. ***(See page 31 for a reproducible blank form.)***

Chapter Four — 27

Record Keeping

• Sample Weekly Work Form

Student Name: Brian   **Week of** October 2, 2000

Skill Area: Fine Motor

Skill:	Trace 10 letters			Copy building a 3-piece model			Lacing cards			Cut along line w/scissors			Fold paper in half		
	Beh.	Perf.	Prog.	Beh.	Perf.	Prog.	Beh.	Perf.	Prog.	Beh.	Perf.	Prog.	Beh.	Perf.	Prog.
MON	+	H	I	+	H	O	-	L	↓	+	L	O	+	N	FT
	could trace A ind.!; also ind. for C,D,L,T,U,V; mixes up stroke order for E; confused for B						*forgot how to pull string through tightly (we hadn't done this for 2 weeks); he got it eventually; some angry noises*			*able to line up scissors nicely for first cut, but not able to make 2nd cut along line*			*did not seem to be figuring out any part of this task*		
TUE															
WED	=	H	O				+	L	I	+	L	O	+	L	I
	started grabbing after having trouble tracing B; prompted him to indicate "don't understand" and simplified the task to tracing P, which he could do						*could do 2 holes in a row independently!*						*tried having him just flatten the paper that I folded over; he could do this!*		
THU	+	H	O	+	H	I				+	L	O	+	L	O
	still some trouble with B, but I prompted him to indicate "don't understand" before he became aggressive			*almost independent! I only needed to help him orient one piece*											
FRI	+	H	O	+	H	O	-	L	O	+	L	O	+	H	I
							angry and did not want to work; he chose "eat", and after a snack he did fine			*still unable to make 2nd cut along line; he looks away and cuts randomly; I will need to come up with some way to have him focus on the paper*			*this time HE folded the paper (on 2nd try) and pressed it flat – edges not lined up though.*		

This is one of three different forms used for tracking data. Choose and use only one of these types of forms (the Weekly Work form, the Single Skill form or the Daily Work form); using more than one type of form results in redundancy and too much paperwork.

The Weekly Work form is similar to the form that I used for tracking data during Brian's second and third year of homeschooling. There is room for tracking five different skills in a particular skill area. One or more of these Weekly Work forms will be needed for each skill area every week. This type of form works well for five-day (Monday–Friday) programs, *e.g.*, school programs.

As one looks down the page, one can see the progress that the student made in each skill (in that skill area) during that week. There are small boxes for noting behavior, performance, and progress. There are larger boxes for comments. ***(See page 33 for a reproducible blank form.)***

Chapter Four

Record Keeping

- **Sample Single Skill Form**

Student Name:	Brian
Skill Area:	Gross Motor
Skill:	walk down stairs alternating feet

Date	Behavior	Performance	Progress	Comment
9/5/00	+	L	FT	can alternate feet as long as he holds on to the rail and I walk ahead of him and gently nudge the back of his leg (at the calf) for each step down.
9/7/00	+	L	O	
9/8/00	+	L	O	
9/11/00	+	L	O	
9/12/00	+	L	I	did 2 steps (alternately) after a single physical prompt; he did this one time
9/14/00	+	L	O	
9/15/00	+	L	O	
9/18/00	+	L	I	did 2 steps (alternately), two times, after a single physical prompt
9/19/00	+	L	O	
9/21/00	+	H	I	able to alternate feet on all steps as long as he holds on to rail and I walk in front of him and I physically prompt him on the first step down; no other physical prompts needed

This is the second of three forms that can be used for tracking data. This is the type of form that I am currently using in Brian's home program. The Single Skill form tracks a single skill in detail. As one looks down the page, one can see the progress that the student made over ten sessions. There are small boxes for noting behavior, performance and progress. There is a large space for a longer comment. One of these Single Skill forms will be needed for each skill that the child is working on. This type of form works best for those teachers who work with a student for only a few days a week, and only work on a few skills.

One of the two disadvantages to this type of form is that there is lots of paperwork involved, so one needs to be well organized to find the proper page quickly. The other drawback is that one needs to remember the day's date (a problem for me). This can be solved by setting a date stamper to the day's date the first thing in the morning and to use it on all the pages (so one doesn't have to keep running into the kitchen to look at the calendar to find out what day it is). Despite this, having room on the page for long comments makes this type of form best for some users. *(See page 35 for a reproducible blank form.)*

Chapter Four

Record Keeping

- **Sample Daily Work Form**

Student Name: **Brian**   Date **October 2, 2000**

Skill Comment	Beh.	Perf.	Prog.	
match picture symbols to photos	−	L	O	didn't want to start
match words	+	H	I	all but one correct
match numerical quantities	+	H	O	
match by size				not done
match objects that belong together				not done
receptive work (with objects)	+	H	O	
receptive work (with photos)	=	L	O	grabbing; several wrong
read to Brian	+			sat quietly
drill weaker areas of communication system	+	L	I	could select "go outside"
spelling (on preschool toy)	+	H	O	
spelling (on computer)	+	H	O	
computer game 1	+	H	O	
computer game 2	+	H	O	
trace 10 letters	+	H	I	could trace A
copy building 3-piece model	+	H	O	
lacing cards	−	L	↓	forgot how to pull string
cut along line w/ scissors	+	L	O	
fold paper in half	+	N	FT	couldn't figure out
walk down stairs alternating feet	+	H	O	
balance on one foot	+	H	I	could do for 5 sec.

Skill Comment	Beh.	Perf.	Prog.	
throw a ball underhand	+	L	O	
broad jump 2'	+	H	I	improved by 4"
music activities	+			showed interest
craft project	+			squeezed glue independently
tolerate new hat	+	H	I	can tolerate for 20 sec.
start zipper	=	N	O	couldn't do; he got angry
snaps	+	H	O	
set table	+	H	O	
put away silverware	+	L	FT	tried for first time
put away plates, bowls, glassware				not done

This is the last of the three forms for tracking data and the type I used during the first year of Brian's home program.

On this form, one writes in all of the skills that the student is working on and then makes multiple copies of this (it wouldn't be practical to write in the skills every day). As the student completes each skill the teacher notes the behavior, performance and progress. There is room for a very brief comment.

The advantage of this type of form is that only one piece of paper is needed over the course of the day. The disadvantages are that there is only room for an extremely brief comment, and, that one cannot readily see the progress the student has made on any skill over a period of time (on that single page).

(See page 37 for a reproducible blank form.)

Planning Form

Student Name:_____   Goals for Year _____

Skill Area: _____

SKILL	INITIAL PROCEDURE/MATERIALS (can indicate one or more alternatives)

START	LOW	HIGH	MASTERED

START	LOW	HIGH	MASTERED

START	LOW	HIGH	MASTERED

START	LOW	HIGH	MASTERED

START	LOW	HIGH	MASTERED

One-on-One

Weekly Work Form

Student Name: _____ Week of _____

Skill Area: _____

Skill:															
	Beh.	Perf.	Prog.	Beh.	Perf.	Prog.	Beh.	Perf.	Prog.	Beh.	Perf.	Prog.	Beh.	Perf.	Prog.
MON															
TUE															
WED															
THU															
FRI															

One-on-One

Single Skill Form

Student Name: _____

Skill Area: _____ Skill _____

Date	Behavior	Performance	Progress	Comment

One-on-One

Daily Work Form

Student Name:_____   **Date** _____

Skill	Beh.	Perf.	Prog.	Comment	Skill	Beh.	Perf.	Prog.	Comment

One-on-One

PART TWO

PART TWO
Some Specific Therapy Ideas

"I don't pretend to understand everything there is to know about autism. I can only hope that underneath it all, Brian really is comprehending everything."

Introduction to Therapy Ideas Section

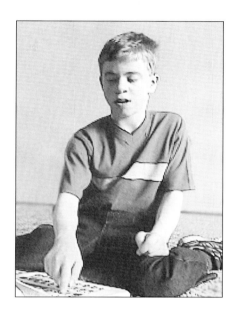

I want to share some observations before we get into the *Therapy Ideas* section, which constitutes the bulk of this book. First of all, I want to point out that these chapters aren't intended to make up a complete program. However, one or more of these approaches may be helpful as an add-on to a child's existing comprehensive program.

The *Matching* and *Communication Skills* chapters are presented sequentially. This is the order in which Brian learned these skills, each building on the previous one. Therefore, if a child hasn't mastered the preceding skills, it's not advisable to begin working with the ideas from one of the later *Matching* or *Communication Skills* chapters. The chapter titled *Beginning to Type Independently* also requires a prerequisite skill: the child must be able to match letters to letters. The other chapters don't require prerequisite skills and can be immediately included as a part of a child's program.

Low level cognitive skills are covered in the *Matching* and *Communication Skills* sections. If any material in these chapters seems to be in contradiction with the idea that Brian may be intelligent...well, so be it. I don't pretend to understand everything there is to know about autism. I can only hope that underneath it all, Brian really is comprehending everything.

I've observed that Brian is frequently unable to learn low level cognitive skills with hand-over-hand prompting or correcting of his response. *(Note: this isn't the case for teaching fine and gross motor skills to Brian. Hand-over-hand prompting, gradually faded, seems to work very well for teaching him these kinds of skills.)* He immediately becomes dependent on the prompts and never figures out what he's supposed to do. He could make the same mistake 100,000 times, and still not figure out the correct response. Conversely, he could be guided to the correct answer 100,000 times and fail to associate it with the question.

What has helped Brian learn low level cognitive skills is breaking down the tasks into such small pieces he can figure out the correct solution to each problem by himself. Then the pieces are built back bit by bit into the original task.

When Brian started to experience success with some cognitive skills, I became aware of the extent to which he hates to be wrong. When he's successful in figuring out a task, he does his work happily. But when he can't figure out what he should be doing, and gets wrong answers, he gets upset and can begin to cry and scream.

The key to knowing if the presentation of a cognitive task is appropriate is simply to observe Brian's reaction. If he's having success and seems happy, then it's the way to go, but if it isn't happening and there's signs of distress, the task needs to be broken down further before continuing. If I don't rethink the problem and present it in a new way, I'm wasting his time and mine.

What helped Brian learn skills, was to break down the tasks into small pieces so he could figure out the solution to each problem by himself. These pieces were then built back one at a time into the original task.

Introduction to Therapy Ideas Section

This contradicts the rule presented earlier that Brian had to complete each task before he could be done with it, no matter how unhappy he might have been. But after we had worked together for over a year and I started to come up with new ways to break down some of the low level cognitive tasks, it became clear that working with Brian on tasks he couldn't understand was useless.

It's worth noting that I don't immediately change the presentation of a cognitive task when Brian is unsuccessful with it on a single trial or over the course of a day. I only change it when we've tried it several times for between two minutes and two hours (however long it takes to convince me he's not going to get it), and he still hasn't grasped what it is he's to do. I won't present the same cognitive task day after day without positive results. On the other hand, I will continue to present fine and gross motor skills, since Brian gets these eventually.

If I continue to present cognitive tasks that Brian is unable to figure out, he starts to form incorrect associations with the materials. So even if he's being complacent and isn't screaming or being aggressive because of incorrect responses, it's still a bad idea to present a task he isn't getting because we waste time unlearning the incorrect associations he's begun to make. It's much better to stop presenting the task, make up new materials and find another way of presenting it before incorrect associations start to form.

Don't fret a brief step backwards

One last observation: when Brian's on the verge of mastering a new cognitive skill, he often goes through a brief period where he alternately forgets and remembers it. During a session, he may be working confidently and happily at 100% accuracy and suddenly drops to 0–30% accuracy and is miserable. When this occurs, I continue working with him until he remembers the skill and is back to 100% (and happy) before quitting. While this can take a while, after a two week period of vacillation, he's very solid with the skill and rarely ever forgets it again. I don't know if other children go through this (extremely frustrating) interim period of having the skill and losing it, but if it happens to your child don't feel alone.

Matching Skills: Picture and Color Matching

Chapter Five

Matching Skills

Breaking Down Picture and Color Matching (into pieces smaller than you can imagine)

Over the years, we tried various picture and color matching methods without success both at home and school. When he was nine, a speech therapist and I worked intensively on picture matching, doing hundreds of thousands of discrete trials over the course of seven months. We'd place two different pictures in front of him and hand him one picture, which he was to place on its match. He'd place it on the wrong picture half of the time. We tried every variation on the discrete trial we could think of, but he wasn't able to figure it out when presented with two pictures. I now realize he was matching the shape of the card, not the picture on it. He thought he was doing it right, and when he was physically prompted or corrected because of choosing the wrong picture, he was surprised and upset.

What eventually helped Brian learn picture matching skills was sorting between pictures and objects involved in completing an easy fine motor task. *(Note: here, the items involved in the two tasks were different enough to allow him to discriminate between them.)* For example, on the table in front of him I'd place a pegboard and a picture of a duck. I then handed him either a peg or an identical picture and he placed the item accordingly. (Note: I'm not referring to the TEACCH pegboard idea mentioned earlier. Here, the pegboard is simply an easy fine motor task with no meaning attached to the giving of each peg.)

Brian eventually learned picture matching skills by sorting between pictures and objects.

Another helpful approach was to hand him multiples (from 5–10) of each item, rather than just a pair. The repetition served to drive the lesson home.

This method can also be used for object matching; just substitute the word "object" for "picture" throughout this chapter.

• Choosing Materials and Tasks

For picture matching, I initially used picture cards from a preschool game that contained multiple images of each. Or you could purchase 3 or 4 identical sets of picture pairs. This would yield 6 or 8 images of each picture.

Chapter Five 43

Matching Skills: Picture and Color Matching

> *Comparing a picture with a color is easier than comparing two pictures or two colors.*

For color matching, I used 4 colored boxes (red, yellow, blue and green), and multiple assorted items red, yellow, blue and green to go into the boxes.

The fine motor tasks I chose were ones Brian could already do easily: putting pegs in a pegboard; stacking blocks together; putting magnets on a steel board; putting small, toy racing cars down their ramp; and putting together a few, easy, wooden inset puzzles.

I also wanted Brian to learn a new task: putting toy farm animals into a barn. Note that all fine motor tasks, easy and new, were motorically very easy; this was not a time to work on complex fine motor skills.

• Definitions

Element — something to be sorted; a picture, a color, or the objects involved in doing a fine motor task. Examples of elements: teddy bear pictures, blue objects, pegs.

Item — a particular piece of what is to be sorted. Examples of individual items: a single teddy bear picture, a blue object, or a peg.

Sorting-group — two or more elements arranged in a specific way (presented exactly the same way each time, until the sorting of the elements in that arrangement is mastered). A sorting-group example: pegs on the right side, teddy bear pictures on the left.

Easy-tasks — fine motor tasks the child has already mastered.

New-tasks — fine motor tasks the child can't do yet.

There are different types of sorting groups, depending on which elements they contain. For example, a picture/easy-task sorting group includes a picture and an easy-task.

The easiest sorting-groups are picture/easy-task, color/easy-task and new-task/easy-task. They're easiest because one element of the sorting-group, the easy-task, is something the child can already do. The first three sorting-groups I'd set up for Brian demonstrated the above three "easy" types. Sorting-group 1 was a picture/easy-task: *i.e.*, large pictures of yellow ducks to be stacked together and pegs to be put in a pegboard. Sorting-Group 2 was a color/easy-task: *i.e.*, red objects to be put in a red box and magnets to be put on a steel board. Sorting-Group 3 was a new-task/easy-task: farm animals to be put into a toy barn and an easy inset puzzle to be completed.

More difficult sorting-group types are: picture/color, color/new-task, and picture/new-task. These are harder because the child is working on two new skills at the same time. But comparing a picture with a color is still easier than comparing two pictures or two colors.

The most difficult types are: picture/picture and color/color. When the child can do these, picture and color matching has been mastered.

Matching Skills: Picture and Color Matching

- ### Sorting-Group Procedure

I initially defined three different sorting-groups. I'd set one up at a time and have Brian sort through all its items. Then I'd clear everything away and set up the next sorting-group and have him complete this, too. He'd complete all three sorting-groups once a day. These were presented in any order: by the second year of his program it was no longer necessary to do every task in the same order.

Gradually, as he experienced more and more success, I added more sorting-groups, each of which was completed once a day.

- ### Record Keeping

I noted the arrangement of each element in each sorting-group on a piece of paper so I could set things up the same way the next day. It was important to keep the elements of a sorting-group in the same position until Brian mastered the specific arrangement.

In addition, I also charted the following designations: "too easy" if a sorting-group should be made a little more difficult; "OK" if it was a challenge but not too frustrating and should be left as is; "too hard" if it was difficult and needed to be simplified.

A sorting-group could be made easier by removing an element from it (if there were more than two), or by separating out each element and working on it individually with easy-tasks before trying to combine them again.

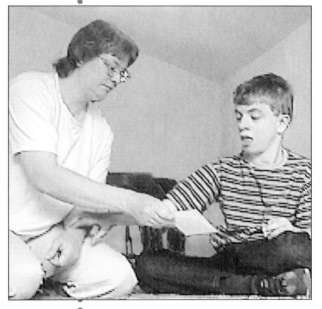

As I handed Brian a picture, I'd say its name in the hope that eventually he'd try to say the word.

Conversely, a sorting-group could be made more difficult by changing the position of elements within it, either by adding easy-tasks, or another picture or color (making the sorting-group more difficult).

- ### Procedure for Handing Items to Brian

As I handed Brian each item, I said its name (*e.g.*, "duck" or "peg"). I did this not because he didn't know what the item was, nor to help or cue him, but in the hope that at some point he'd try to say the word.

Before I go into more detail on how I'd hand Brian the items, let's look at some ideas from the book, *From Ritual to Repertoire*, by A. Miller and E. Eller-Miller. The Millers define "spheres" as "deliberately established repetitive sequences,"[2] which are "introduced by a worker."[3] According to the Millers, this "interruption of a sphere results in the child's compensatory tendency to continue this activity,"[4] thus they recommend that "the worker interrupt at a point of maximal tension."[5]

The idea is, if you disturb the child's routine at the height of his interest, rather than after he's done numerous repetitions and has become bored, when you return to it he'll pick up where he left off, at a high interest level.

I embraced the Millers' "repetition/interruption" approach[6] for handing Brian items for sorting-groups. I didn't hand him items randomly, but rather would hand

Chapter Five

Matching Skills: Picture and Color Matching

Figure 2 Sorting-Group 1– pictures were stacked together and pegs were put in a pegboard.

him as many of the same item as he needed until he was able to start putting it in its proper place. When he had placed one or two (or sometimes three) of the same item correctly and independently, I decided that he was at the height of his interest in this activity and "interrupted" the process by handing him the other item. Again, I repetitively handed him the second item until he started putting it in its proper place. When he had placed one, two or three of the second item correctly and independently, I "interrupted" and handed him the first item again. I continued in this manner until I finished handing him all of the items for that sorting-group.

• Response to Correct Placement of an Item

When Brian placed an item correctly, he got verbal praise; no food or toy reinforcers, etc. Doing a task correctly was reinforcement enough. He was always pleased with himself for figuring out what to do. In addition, he rarely got bored doing a skill, because he was always interrupted well before he got to that point.

A therapist trained in ABA once pointed out that Brian's reward for a good performance on harder tasks was switching to an easier and more agreeable task. And in the meantime, he also got in a little extra practice on the easier task.

• Response to Incorrect Placement of an Item

If Brian placed an item incorrectly, I responded in one of two ways, depending on whether it was a new skill, or one he had previously done well but now was doing incorrectly. If it was a new skill, I tried to help him find the correct location of the item, usually by pointing to it. If this was insufficient, then I used hand-over-hand prompting to place the item correctly.

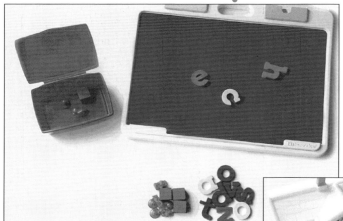

Figure 3 Sorting-Group 2 –red objects were put into a red box and magnets were put on a steel board.

Figure 4 Sorting-Group 3 — farm animals were put into a toy barn and an easy inset puzzle was to be completed.

Chapter Five

Matching Skills: Picture and Color Matching

For a skill he'd previously done well, but was now doing incorrectly, I allowed one error in placing an item, and helped him to correct himself via pointing and hand-over-hand prompting. However, if I had to help Brian correct himself 2 or 3 times in a row, I'd pick up all the items for that activity and say "let's do this again." I then had him sort the items again, from the beginning, as many times as necessary, until he started independently putting them in their correct place.

- **Criteria for Sorting-Group Mastery**

When Brian could switch back and forth quickly between two or more elements without a problem (*i.e.*, I'd hand the items to him randomly, rather than repetitively, and he placed them correctly with 100% accuracy), then I considered him to have mastered that sorting-group. When he achieved mastery with a sorting-group, it would be increased in difficulty. However, if doing the sorting-group frustrated him, then I simplified the situation. I wouldn't continue to ask him to do something he couldn't handle.

- **Specific Details of How Brian Mastered Picture Matching**

The three sorting-groups we started with were:

1. large pictures of yellow ducks to be stacked together and pegs to be put in a pegboard (see Figure 2);

2. red objects to be put in a red box and magnets to be put on a steel board (see Figure 3);

3. farm animals to be put into a toy barn and an easy inset puzzle to be completed (see Figure 4).

Sorting-Group 1: first, I handed Brian as many duck pictures as is necessary until he initiated putting them on the pile correctly by himself. (Usually ten cards, but if I ran out I grabbed some off the pile.) Then, I interrupted the duck sequence to hand him a peg. Since pegs are easy for him, it took only two to four before he was doing it well. At this point, I interrupted the peg sequence and went back to handing him duck cards, until I'd handed him all the cards and pegs. We then completed Sorting-Groups 2 and 3 in a similar manner.

After one or two tries with Sorting-Group 1 (pegs and duck cards), I added another easy-task to the sorting-group: stacking blocks. I did this because pegs are easy, and he was able to handle more of a challenge. That gave him three elements to sort amongst: pegs, duck cards and blocks. When I set up this sorting-group, I put the pegboard, cards, and the first block in the same place. I learned if I switched things around at this point, it made it too difficult for Brian and he would start to show signs of frustration (see Figure 5).

Figure 5 *If things were switched around, it was too difficult for Brian and he would show signs of frustration.*

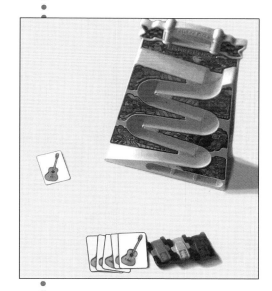

Figure 6 *In the fourth sorting-group, I introduced a second large picture card of a blue guitar and small racing cars to be put on a track.*

Chapter Five

Matching Skills: Picture and Color Matching

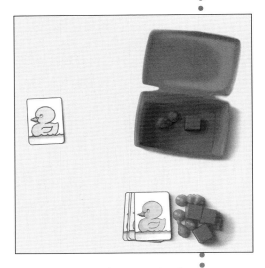

Figure 7 Within a week of changing the picture/color type set, Brian was able to easily sort between duck cards and red objects.

Figure 8 At two weeks into the program, Brian was able to sort farm animals and colored objects accurately.

Three days into the program I introduced a second large picture card as a fourth sorting-group. I chose a card distinct from the yellow duck, *e.g.,* a blue guitar card. Sorting-Group 4 was a picture/easy-task type: blue guitar cards were to be stacked on top of each other and small racing cars were to be put down on their track. I didn't put blue guitar cards in the same sorting-group as yellow duck cards (see Figure 6).

Four days into the program, Brian's was doing so well with Sorting-Group 1, I decided to make it more difficult. I changed it to a picture/color type: yellow duck cards and red objects. He tried repeatedly to put duck cards in the red box and red items on the pile of duck cards. It made me think, if he couldn't sort between a colored object and a picture, no wonder he couldn't sort between two pictures! But within a week, he was able to easily sort between duck cards and red objects (see Figure 7).

During the first week and a half, he made progress with all four sorting-groups. I was able to introduce a third and fourth large picture card into the two sorting-groups that didn't have cards. I also introduced blue and yellow boxes, with each color being in a separate sorting-group.

Two weeks into the program, I tried another type that was more difficult: color/new-task. I began by having Brian sort between the farm animals going into a barn and blue objects going into a blue box. (The barn was red, so I didn't use the red box.) Previously we had worked on both these skills separately. Putting them together proved to be too difficult. Brian got many wrong and showed signs of frustration. Both tasks involved tossing a 3-D object into a container, but they were too similar. I separated the tasks back into sorting-groups for a week and tried combining them again. The second time around, he was able to sort farm animals and blue objects accurately without a problem (see Figure 8).

Two weeks into the program, Brian was easily and accurately stacking cards together in each of the sorting-groups, so we moved on to comparing two pictures. Rather than comparing two large picture cards, I decided to have him compare a large card (yellow duck) to a small card (red apple). (Previously I'd introduced the red apple card in a sorting-group that didn't have large picture cards—see Figure 9.)

The small picture card was half the size of the duck card, making the comparison easier. But, I only had two of each of the small cards, so it was impossible to stack the cards repetitively, if that had been necessary. But as it turned out, he was able to sort between the duck and apple cards without a problem. Promptly I introduced other small picture cards in other sorting-groups. *(Note: I always used the same cards until he was familiar with them and did them well.)*

Chapter Five

Matching Skills: Picture and Color Matching

Three weeks into the program, I tried having Brian compare two large picture cards—the yellow duck and the blue guitar. He did it. In fact, his accuracy was about 70–80%.

Two observations about Brian's early matching skills:

1. he was able to sort the cards well when they were about eight inches apart, but when they were too close (one inch) or too far apart (one foot), he was unable to sort them;
2. separating the two large picture cards by a small picture card (or a small task, *e.g.,* a narrow pegboard) seemed to help. Over the next few weeks, these "helps" were no longer necessary (see Figure 10).

Gradually, I put out more of the small and large picture cards and fewer easy-tasks until there were no tasks at all with the cards. At this point, the sorting-groups with picture cards are all picture/picture types.

At about seven weeks into the program, Brian was able to sort four large picture cards with 100% accuracy. At this point, I'd mostly stopped using large cards, because they were too easy and he was sorting six small picture cards with 90% accuracy (see Figure 11). Before long he started to generalize sorting first to the rest of the small picture cards, then to other picture cards, and finally to letter and number cards. Brian is now able to match sixteen small picture cards at a time (four rows, four columns).

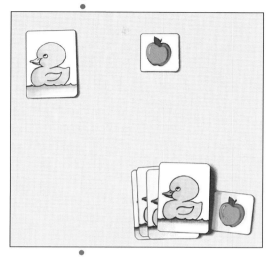

Figure 9 Brian had no problem sorting two picture cards of different sizes.

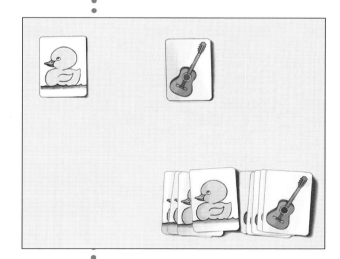

Figure 10 Brian's early matching skills proved that the distance between the pictures affected his ability to be able to match them.

Figure 11 At seven weeks into the program, Brian was able to match a number of small picture cards.

Chapter Five

Matching Skills: Picture and Color Matching

> *When I teach color matching, I'm careful not to create ambiguous situations by handing Brian items that can be used in two places. For example, if a sorting-group has a red box for red items and a pegboard for colored pegs, I make sure not to hand him a red peg. Because a red peg could go in either the red box or the pegboard, handing it to him causes confusion and frustration, so I put it aside.*

• Color Matching

On the third and fourth weeks of the matching program I ran into a problem when I introduced 4 color boxes (red, blue, yellow, green), each in a separate sorting-group. Since at this point Brian was starting to be able to match pictures, I reasoned that color matching would soon follow. But this wasn't the case. While he was able to successfully put colored items (one-inch colored blocks and small plastic dinosaurs) into their boxes when they were in separate sorting-groups, when I put two colored boxes together in the same sorting-group he got many wrong and was very frustrated. At first I thought he just needed more time to practice doing them separately. But after two more weeks of separate practice, the results were still the same when I put two colors together.

It occurred to me that he wasn't looking at the objects thoroughly, since putting colored objects in the boxes required a "tossing" action, while matching picture cards involved a more careful, scanning motion. So I eliminated colored boxes and had him place the pieces on matching colored construction paper. But after two weeks, it was clear this wasn't going to work either.

I thought it was confusing for him that the objects weren't all the same shape. I determined that all objects should be of the same dimensions, so I bought 4 dozen small wooden spools at a craft store and painted them blue, red, yellow and green—a dozen of each color. I asked Brian to sort them on to the colored paper (two colors at a time) and also into the colored boxes. Still no luck.

About this time, a consultant who was starting to help with Brian's program suggested I make some cards out of colored construction paper and see if he was able to match them. I cut the paper the same size as the large picture cards, ten of each color and put 2 color cards out at a time for him to sort (see Figure 12). He was immediately able to sort all of these different combinations at 80–90% accuracy. This meant he was able to recognize color! But he could only sort colored 2-D objects and not 3-D objects.

So I tried to make the 3-D objects look 2-D. First, I realized the 3-D colored objects I was using were too small. When Brian held them, they disappeared in his hand leaving little for him to see. Next, I cut out four-inch diameter circles from blue, red, yellow and green construction paper, a dozen of each color. I glued them to the bottom of the colored spools and had Brian group them onto matching pieces of colored construction paper (only 2 colors at a time). He still had trouble with this, but I persisted, since I couldn't think of any other way to break the task down any further. After a week and a half, it clicked.

Over the next few weeks, I cut paper circles into medium, small, very small, until finally we were using no paper, just spools and he was successful at matching all of these! (See Figure 13a–d).

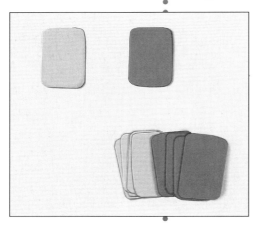

Figure 12 *Using colored construction paper cut to the same size as the large picture cards, Brian was able to recognize color but could only sort two dimensional objects.*

Matching Skills: Picture and Color Matching

With a little practice, Brian was soon able to match other different colored objects, as long as I only put out objects of the same shape (*e.g.,* colored blocks only). He wasn't able to sort a mixed group of objects by color until about a month later.

Looking back at color matching, I could have done some things better. When I started working with the colored spools, I should have introduced each color separately in different sorting-groups paired with easy-tasks. Instead I jumped right into color/color work. We no longer used sorting-groups, but just did drills for hours a day with two colors out. This caused a lot of frustration, although eventually he did figure it out.

A suggestion for those trying this method: since a child may be able to work better with 2-D objects as opposed to 3-D (or *vice versa*), it may be a good idea to try a variety of different colored materials in the sorting-groups right from the start to see what works best. For example, try 2-D colored cards as well as colored boxes. Colored spools with paper circles attached (or something similar) might also be good items for the child to start sorting with; they are a good 2-D / 3-D compromise. Make sure all objects being sorted by color are identical in shape.

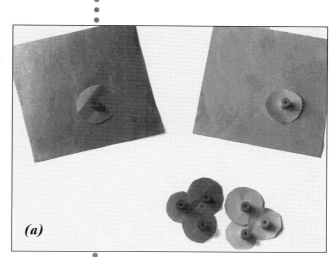
(a)

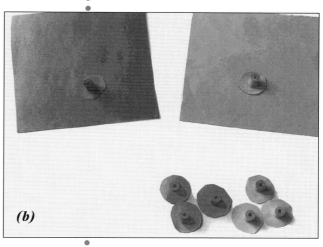
(b)

Figure 13 *Making three dimensional objects look more like two dimensional objects, Brian was able to match the objects after a week and a half.*

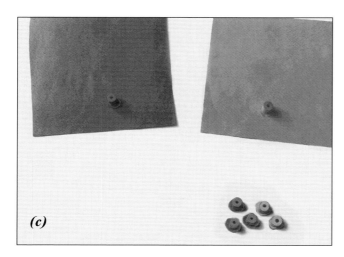
(c)

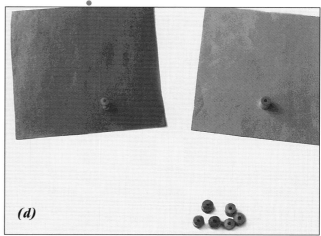
(d)

Chapter Five

Matching Skills: Picture and Color Matching

• Shape Matching

Another skill Brian learned was sorting shapes. We worked on this after he had learned picture and color matching.

I cut out multiples of 8 different shapes from black poster board, and had Brian sort (shape/shape) starting with 2 shapes and working up to 6 at a time. Using black for shapes, rather than a variety of colors, was suggested in *The ME Book*, by Ivar Lovaas.[7] (See Figure 14). This was a good idea because I didn't want to confuse Brian by making him sort different colored items by shape after everything he learned about color matching. Happily, he was able to sort all of the black shapes immediately. Thank goodness not everything has been difficult.

I could have introduced black shapes in the sorting-groups right from the start and worked on shape matching as well as picture and color matching right away. But, I hadn't thought of it at the time. As it turned out, after acquiring picture and color matching skills, Brian was able to match the shapes instantly without much additional work. It's possible this may happen for other children, too, but I can't say for sure.

Figure 14 *After Brian learned picture and color matching, he learned to sort different shapes cut from black poster board.*

Matching Skills: Complex Picture Matching

Complex Picture Matching

Having mastered picture, color, and shape matching, next we tried to match pairs of pictures and photos with complex backgrounds. To my surprise, since he was able to match large and small picture cards with ease and could easily match photos of single objects, he had difficulty with this.

The difference between the tasks was that the backgrounds on the complex pictures were cluttered, while they were plain white on picture cards. The white backgrounds highlighted the objects and made them easier for him to recognize.

Two things finally helped Brian learn to match pairs of complex pictures and photos. The first was additional practice. In time, he was able to match most complex pictures, without extra help.

However, he never seemed to be able to figure out a few of them. For these, I simplified the task by making a third copy of the picture and cutting out the main object. Then I had him match the cut-out object to its correct place on the complex picture (see Figure 15). When he could do this, I went back to having him match complex picture to complex picture. After this, he was able to recognize the whole picture.

• Other Picture Matching Ideas

Here are a few other suggestions for improving picture matching skills. The first two are mine, while others are from a consultant who was helping with Brian's program.

Figure 15 *Matching cut-out main objects to complex pictures.*

1. Student matches black-and-white line drawings.
2. Student matches numbers, letters or words.
3. Student matches black-and-white pictures to their colored counterparts. (Simply make black-and-white photocopies of colored pictures.) Do this for simple pictures (*i.e.,* single objects with white backgrounds) and complex pictures (*i.e.,* pictures with cluttered backgrounds).
4. Student matches similar pictures of different sizes (see Figure 16). (To do this, shrink or enlarge copies with a photocopier—black-and-white or color.)
5. Student matches cut-out colored main object to the correct place on the black-and-white photocopy of the complex picture (see Figure 17). (To do this, make a black-and-white photocopy of the complex picture—if there's a color-copy of the main object.)

Chapter Five

Matching Skills: Object to Photo (Picture) Matching

I either had color copies made, or for photos I had reprints made. It's also possible to make color copies of photos. To save money, have a number of pictures and photos color-copied together

Figure 16 *Matching smaller, complex pictures to larger complex pictures.*

Figure 17 *Matching colored cut-out main objects to black-and-white photocopies.*

Matching Skills: Object to Photo (Picture) Matching

Object to Photo (Picture) Matching

After Brian started having success matching pictures, I introduced object to picture matching. I felt it was necessary for him to have picture to picture and object to object matching skills first. I don't recommend working on object to picture matching with a child until he has these other skills in place.

I already had a set of small objects that came with matching picture cards. The pictures were accurate representations of the objects, almost photographic. So Brian actually was learning object to photo rather than object to picture matching, which is more abstract and difficult.

The cards also contained object names, but at this point these were unnecessary. From this set of materials, I only used objects that fit on the cards without overlap.

I selected five object/photo pairs, and we worked on these one at a time, once a day. Brian would work on a particular object/photo pair until he had correctly and independently placed the object on the photo once and he was done with it for the day. Then we would go on to the next object/photo pair. When Brian placed an object incorrectly, I would help him by pointing to the photo on the card or by assisting him hand-over-hand. Then he would try it again (and again) until he placed the object correctly and independently once. He had a lot of difficulty learning this skill. He often put the object on the word that was on the card, or he didn't put it on the card at all. He didn't see the connection between an object and its photo for a long time—two months to be exact. But, all of a sudden it clicked, and I was able to start putting out two object/photo pairs, then three, etc. I was also able to introduce new object/photo pairs.

I wasn't too worried about how long it took, because my main concern was for him to learn color matching skills. At the time, he was working on them concurrently. He learned object to photo matching soon after color matching.

There's a different and perhaps better way to teach this skill, an approach used with two children who had great difficulty learning to match objects to pictures or photos. After using the following object to photo matching approach, one child learned the skill in three days, the other child learned it in one session: substitute multiples (four to six) of objects and photos for object/photo pairs. Using multiples of objects and photos yields faster results than pairs, because the child gets in a lot more practice. Place a set of identical photos (four to six) on a desk or table, laying the cards face up. Hand the child the objects that match the photos. Do this repeatedly, helping him place each object correctly on its photo. For example, put four identical photos of a clothespin in front of the child. Hand him four clothespins, one at a time, and help him place one on each of the four photos (see Figure 18). Follow the same procedure with the other sets of identical photos. Don't mix photo sets. For example, after the child completes the exercise of matching clothespins to their photos, clear them away and put out a set of four identical photos of a gift bow. Have the child match four bows to these photos (see

> ### *Excellent Product Alert*
>
> ### *Pockets Matching System*
> A great product for building on matching skills is the *Pockets Matching System*. Using it, the child progresses from identical matching to categorization and on to understanding words that represent categories or concepts. For a catalog or to order by phone:
>
> *Maddak Inc.*
> *Pequannock, NJ*
> *07440-1993*
> *800-443-4926*

Matching Skills: Object to Photo (Picture) Matching

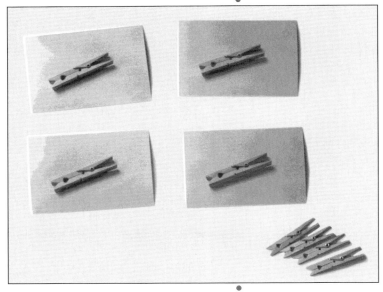

Figure 18 Matching clothespins to their photos.

Figure 19 Matching bows to their photos.

Figure 19). Don't put clothespin and bow photos together quite yet. It's likely the child isn't ready for this. At this point, you simply want him to notice that each set of photos looks a little different from the other sets.

A potential problem at this point in the learning curve occurs when the child tries to group objects together rather than placing them on the photos, since he can already do object to object matching. The child will probably need hand-over-hand help or pointing to the photo, to place the object correctly.

A second potential problem occurs when the child has trouble spotting the last one or two "empty" photos, and tries to put the object on a photo that's already occupied. If he's becoming frustrated because of this, try using only two or three photos at first, rather than five or six.

Gradually try to mix placing objects on their photos with doing additional easy tasks. For example, make up a sorting-group that consists of photos of clothespins, with the clothespins to be put on the photos, and a magnet board with magnets. Using the "repetition/interruption" concept[8], hand the child clothespins or magnets to place appropriately (see Figure 20).

When he can quickly and accurately place objects on photos in all separate sorting-groups, abandon this way

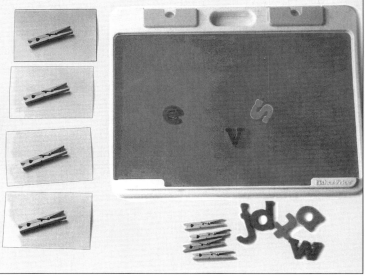

Figure 20 Mixing object to photo matching with an easy task such as placing magnets.

Matching Skills: Object to Photo (Picture) Matching

of teaching the skill. The reason for ceasing the "sorting-group" method and going on to conventional drills is that it's overwhelming to combine and present the materials of two sorting-groups (with eight to twelve photos and eight to twelve objects). It's more manageable to go back to conventional drills and present only two different photos.

Put out two different photos (of objects introduced in the sorting-groups) and see if the child is able to place objects correctly. For example, put out a photo of a clothespin and a gift bow (see Figure 22). Do this a number of times, using different combinations of two different photos. If the child is able to place two objects correctly, then gradually put out three, then four, five and six photos at a time. If he's successful with these, it's possible he may have generalized the skill and can pick up new object/photo pairs with little difficulty. However, it may be that he can accurately match initial sets of objects and photos, but still needs new objects introduced via the sorting-group method.

On the other hand, if the child does well when photos are in separate sorting-groups, but can't do it when two different photos are placed together, additional intermediate steps may be necessary to help him bridge the gap.

Middle- and high-functioning children will probably be able to work successfully with picture symbols rather than photos and initially a

Figure 21 *Mixing object to photo matching with an easy task such as placing pegs in a pegboard.*

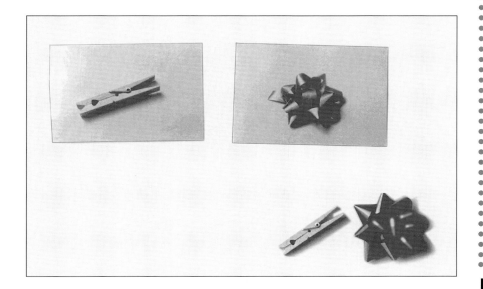

Figure 22 *Matching an object to a photo of the object using two different objects.*

Chapter Five

Matching Skills: Object to Photo (Picture) Matching

Assembling the materials for this method may be a bit costly, but objects don't have to be expensive. Locate five or six sets of small, ordinary household objects – e.g., clothespins, paper clips, spoons, pencils – and make a photo or picture of one item in each set. In addition, make four to six copies of the photo or picture.

set of these pictures will need to be purchased. Of course, this is less of a problem for schools than for parents.

Low-functioning children will likely need to work from photographs. Depending on your means, you can acquire a set photos or take your own. If you choose the latter option, I recommend acquiring a decent 35mm camera to take in-focus, close-up object photos. Picture symbols are too abstract for the low-functioning child to recognize with any consistency, until he is further along with his skills.

Whether you opt to do your own photography, or purchase a set of picture symbols, both will come into use later when you make a picture/photo communication notebook and picture/photo schedule. Believe me, I have taken many photos!

Photography Tips

For best results, always use a 35mm (or digital camera). Then place the object to be photographed on white poster board. If it's small, four inches or less, use a 2X converter, or the object will appear too small in the photo. Move the camera close enough to the object to fill most of the viewfinder. Follow directions included with the camera for setting shutter speed and F-stop and experiment with lighting conditions to find out what works best. My optimal condition is indoors on a sunny day with adequate light. Don't place the object where direct sunlight is streaming into the room, because this will cast a shadow. Also, stay away from fluorescent lights as the photos will have a greenish hue.

Chapter Five

Chapter Six

Receptive Skills

Receptive Labeling

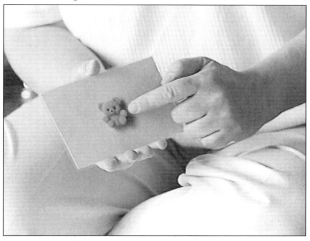

To teach receptive labeling, I would place objects in front of Brian and say the name of one object while holding out its photo.

Receptive labeling is the ability to match objects to their spoken names. For example, if I place a comb and a toothbrush in front of Brian and say, "comb" Brian must point to the comb to demonstrate this skill.

Let me start by saying that my first attempt at teaching this skill to Brian did not work. Nor did my second attempt, or my third, fourth, or fifteenth. One of my favorite sayings, which applies here, is by Thomas Edison, "Now we know 800 ideas that don't work."

Persistence and trying many promising ideas seems to be the key to success with teaching skills to Brian. It's extremely rare that an idea works in its original form. Of course, I always think it will. When I have a new idea, I'm always optimistic: "Oh, this is such a good idea, it will work." But it usually doesn't. Autism is a tough problem. I mention this because many people give up on teaching a skill to a child after trying one or two approaches. But it may take anywhere up to 25 different angles to solve the problem.

My first idea for teaching receptive labeling to Brian was to use object photos as cues. I'd put two or three objects in front of Brian and say the name of one while holding out its photo. I helped him point to the correct object several times, and he quickly caught on that he was supposed to point to the object on the photo. He did this with 100% accuracy. Over several practice hours (not on the same day), I gradually faded the photo cue. However, if I would completely fade it out, he had absolutely no idea which object to point to. However briefly, he still needed to see the photo to find the correct object. My words were meaningless to him.

Next I tried "animating" the objects. I wish I had a set of objects that would say their names when Brian touched them. (In fact, this technology exists and I hope some company will release a product like this in the near future.) In any event, I didn't have a set of talking objects, so I did the talking myself. Whenever Brian touched an object he was working with, I would say its name. He caught on quickly and liked it when I did this. He would repeatedly point to an object, and I would say its name over and over again, as if I were some sort of electronic toy. I tried flashing the object's photo as I said its name, but I decided that was a distraction and stopped doing it.

My first attempts to teach Brian receptive labeling reminded me of what Thomas Edison said, "Now we know 800 ideas that don't work."

Receptive Skills

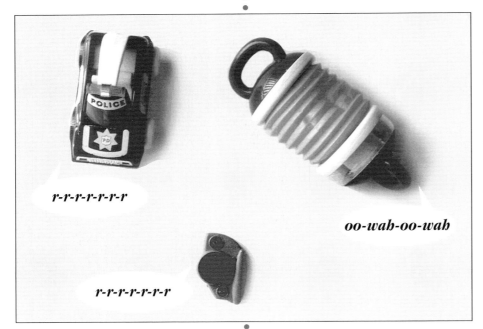

r-r-r-r-r-r-r

oo-wah-oo-wah

r-r-r-r-r-r-r

Figure 23 *Matching the sounds made by these toys. (Brian could not do this).*

ting-ting

shooka-shooka

clack-clack

clack-clack

Figure 24 *Matching the sounds made by musical instruments. (Brian **could** do this).*

After practicing this for 10-15 minutes, I tried to get Brian to point to one of the objects when I said its name. It didn't click for him, and it still didn't after continuing in this manner for several hours. However, this exercise of naming the object as he pointed to it (as well as having the object say its own name) proved to be helpful later on in our work when it came to Brian's success in differentiating the sounds of two words.

• Distinguishing Sounds

Next, I decided to see if Brian could distinguish between two non-word sounds. I bought four devices that record and play back a single short message and were identical in color. Then, I recorded the sounds of three of Brian's toys on separate devices. These included: a police car that makes a siren sound, a toy accordion that makes a musical sound, and a toy bus that says, "buckle up, here we go." (See Figure 23).

Next, I put two toys in front of Brian and pressed the play button on one device to play a toy sound. Then I helped Brian make the correct toy repeat the sound. He soon realized he was supposed to make each toy produce its sound after I made the sound on the recording device. However, he was never able to distinguish between the sounds of any two toys. I tried positional prompting, holding the recording device close to the toy he was supposed to choose. Also I tried letting him press the play button on the recording device, since he seemed to want to do this. I suspect this didn't work for him because he had "stimmed" on these toys for years and that might have made it difficult for him to use them meaningfully.

The next approach I used for teaching receptive labeling came from a therapist, who suggested shaking a maraca out of Brian's view to try to get him to copy it. It sounded promising and I had a pair at home so I put together a "sound" sorting-group of musical instruments. I bought duplicates of the cheapest musical instruments with distinct sounds that I could find. They were: wood blocks and sticks and finger cymbals. I used them in addition to my pair of maracas.

I placed two different instruments in front of Brian, and played one that matched one within his view. He soon realized he was supposed to copy the sound using the instrument that matched the one I played (see Figure 24). Before long, I was able to move my instruments behind my back and

Chapter Six

Receptive Skills

play them out of his sight. His responses were accurate. The few times he was incorrect, I brought the instrument into full view, played it in front of him, and he quickly corrected his mistake. Within two days he could match the sounds of the three instruments in front of him (in any order) with 100% accuracy!

The TEACCH pegboard strategy (*see Chapter Three, Expanding the Program*) was helpful in teaching this skill. It worked because it solved a basic problem: it made it clear to Brian when he was done with his work. The problem was, unlike most of the other sorting-groups, this one had no logical end point. In theory, I could ask him to identify a thousand sounds without stopping, and I don't think he would have been very happy about this. To show him when he was finished, I used a 10 hole pegboard (see Figure 25). Each time Brian gave a correct, independent response, he got a peg to put in the pegboard. When it was filled, I helped him sign "done" and let him leave. He caught on to this concept quickly. Soon he was signing on his own and leaving when he saw the pegs were in.

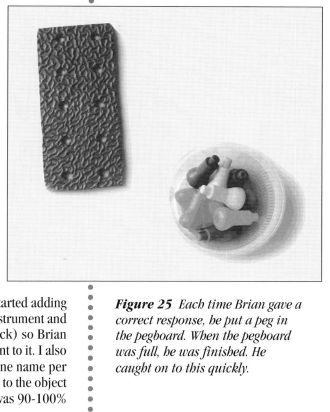

Figure 25 Each time Brian gave a correct response, he put a peg in the pegboard. When the pegboard was full, he was finished. He caught on to this quickly.

When Brian became accurate at distinguishing instrument sounds, I started adding some words. I created sorting-groups consisting of a single musical instrument and an object. I would either play the musical instrument (behind my back) so Brian would copy its sound, or say the name of the object and help Brian point to it. I also recorded myself saying names of objects on the recording devices (one name per device), and played these for him (again, behind my back). He'd point to the object when he heard its name on the recording. Within a few days, Brian was 90-100% accurate with these sorting-groups.

In addition, I added a second musical instrument to each of the sorting-groups so they now consisted of two musical instruments and one object. Brian sorted these sounds at 90-100% accuracy within a day.

Chapter Six

Receptive Skills

The sorting-group idea worked fine as long as I didn't add a second object. If I tried to put two objects together, for example, a comb and a toothbrush, Brian couldn't sort between their sounds and would become quickly frustrated. It was as if the English language was meaningless noise to him.

• Objects that say their names

Next, I came up with a way of making objects say their names. I attached each object to a recording device so when Brian pressed the object, the play button was activated and said its name. (See Figure 26). This gave Brian good auditory feedback.

Figure 26

Making objects that say their names

I used strapping tape to attach objects to the recording device. Here's an example: I taped a screw to the end of a comb, so its head stuck out about a half inch. Then I taped the head of the screw on top of the play button. I elevated the comb a quarter inch by placing it on a pegboard strip. I didn't elevate the recording device. When Brian pressed down on the top half of the comb, the screw made contact with the play button and the pre-recorded word comb played.

> *I began to see a glimmering of hope. Brian was beginning to recognize that words were different. I don't think he was associating the words with objects, but at least he had an inkling that they were different*

This worked well, but it didn't help Brian differentiate between the words for any two objects. He still couldn't press down on the correct object when I said its name, even after repeated practice.

So next I tried the repetition/interruption approach *(see Chapter Five, Picture and Color Matching, pg. 45)*. Since it usually took Brian a while to "get in the groove," I would do seven to ten trials with one object (*e.g.*, a comb) before switching to the other (a toothbrush). Then I did seven to ten trials with the second object before switching back to the first. The work was complete when I observed one or more successful switches on Brian's part: *i.e.*, he independently recognized I had switched from saying "comb" to "toothbrush" or *vice versa*.

Using this switching method, I started to see glimmerings of hope. Brian was beginning to recognize that "toothbrush" and "comb" were different words, because he often switched correctly between them. I don't think he was necessarily associating words with objects, but at least he had an inkling they were different sounds.

There was a problem I began to notice while doing this work: Brian often anticipated my command and pressed the object before I said its word. Also,

Chapter Six

frequently when I said a word, he didn't respond. This probably stemmed from the fact that he had been ignoring my words for so many years. Why, suddenly, should he start paying attention to them now? In Applied Behavioral Analysis terminology, Brian wasn't recognizing the words as the "discriminative stimulus."

To solve this problem, I used hand-over-hand prompting to help Brian respond quickly to the command (discriminative stimulus). In addition, I required him to rest his hand on his knee until I gave the command. This approach helped him understand the word I spoke was a command, and afterwards he usually responded in timely fashion. However, the hand-over-hand prompting didn't help him to correctly associate the words with the objects. Once Brian realized the words I said were commands, I stopped using hand-over-hand because he never seemed to like it.

With two objects out (the comb and the toothbrush) and the recording devices attached, Brian was starting to do well. At first, I kept the objects in the same positions. Then I tried switching them around. Brian couldn't deal with this and responded as if they hadn't been moved. He was associating a position in space with each word, but not the object itself. I became aware that he didn't look at the objects when he pressed them, so was never able to form an association between object and its corresponding word. This was another major problem.

Brian makes a request on one of his communication devices.

To get Brian to look at objects, I used copies of each object. I'd hold the duplicate copy in the air but close to its match (which was hooked up to a recorder). Brian would touch the duplicate while I said its name. *(Note: I mentioned this idea earlier when I talked about "animating" objects. Brian had to look at the object because I held it in the air and it wasn't always in the same place. In fact, if Brian was reaching for an object I held but wasn't looking at it, I'd deliberately move it around so he was forced to look at the object to find it.)*

I'd have Brian point to the duplicate several times and when he did I'd say its name. Then I'd put the duplicate behind my back, pause briefly, and say the name of the object as a command, expecting him to press down on the correct object attached to one of the recorders. He quickly figured out this cue. At this point, he was finally starting to look at the objects attached to the recording devices.

We worked intensively on two pairs of objects: a comb and a toothbrush, and a spoon and a toy truck. Each had a recorder attached (which spoke its name when pressed). While I used duplicates to get Brian to look at the actual objects, I gradually faded their use for cueing as he started to look more consistently at the originals attached to the recorders. However, when he reached for an incorrect object, I still used duplicates for cueing. I used the repetition/interruption concept for switching and gradually moved to totally random switching. I made sure to change the position of the objects frequently, so Brian wouldn't associate the words with positions in space. Following this plan, over a two day period his accuracy when working with any two of the four objects (in any position) was 90-100%.

Receptive Skills

To help Brian recognize more objects, I had him use them in a functional manner rather than having him point to them.

Next we worked with three of the four objects. We tried for several days, in the manner described in the previous paragraph, but he had little success. If I used any sort of a pattern while saying the names of the three objects, Brian would figure it out and his rate of correct responses would improve to over 50%. But if I said the names of the objects in random order, he only got 10-20% correct. When there were two objects out, Brian could localize the sounds to the two different positions, but with three it was just too complicated for him. Apparently, he still hadn't attached the names to the objects themselves.

My next thought was perhaps I wasn't rewarding him properly so he couldn't figure out if he had responded correctly, and hence wasn't able to connect the name to the actual object.

I went back to using the pegboard idea from TEACCH. Each time he got a correct response on the first try, he got a peg. If he made an incorrect response, I'd cue him to get a correct one. Then I'd repeat the same word as many times as necessary until he gave an independent correct response. He wouldn't earn a peg for this response (as he had previously). Instead, I'd simply say, "good," and pause before going on to the next word. He finds "good" rewarding and it's not confusing for him as long as I pause before saying the next word. I had always been concerned about using verbal praise, because I knew it might confuse him, and up until this point, I used it sparsely.

When all ten pegs were in the board, he was done with the session. By using the pegboard in this manner, he was clear about when he was correct. In addition, he wasn't done with the work as quickly (unless he really knew what he was doing), and so when the session was complete, I felt we had accomplished something.

However, even with this reward scheme, Brian still wasn't able to work well with three objects (recording devices attached).

So I decided to give hand-over-hand prompting another try. Perhaps I hadn't given it a fair chance, being somewhat biased against it. After all, it works well for many children. But after trying it for a total of nine hours (not all on the same day) using the same three objects in the same positions, Brian still couldn't consistently match one object to its name. (I used three objects because Brian could now localize the sounds from two different positions and figure out the labels of any two objects after a few trials.)

Next, I used objects that were more familiar to Brian, including some of his favorite toys. We started with three toys, no recorders attached. Initially, his accuracy was a bit better than 50%. But with repeated work, I didn't feel he was doing all that much better than with the objects we had been using.

• **Attaching words to objects**

I thought perhaps Brian had a fundamental problem with attaching words (sounds) to objects (nouns). Maybe his brain wasn't up to making these kinds of connections. After all, I couldn't think of a single instance where I was sure he knew the name of a object. (He was eleven years old at the time.) With all this work, he could differentiate between the sounds of two words. But no matter what I tried, he was unable to connect the words with the objects.

But Brian was able to understand several verbs, or commands. For example, he learned the command "wave goodbye." He reacted appropriately to: "sit down," "stand up," "put this in [the box]," and "turn on/off the light." He could even understand the phrases, "use your handkerchief" and "put your handkerchief in your pocket." (We had previously worked extensively on this skill.)

I decided to put out a handkerchief with two other objects to see if Brian could recognize it. He could. When I said, "handkerchief," he selected it with 80% accuracy. But instead of pointing to it, he would either pick it up and wipe his nose with it, or put it in his pocket. He treated the noun handkerchief as a command, or a noun plus a verb.

But it gave us a starting point. Brian knew one noun by name and he knew it by associating it with an action. Keeping in mind this idea of making objects more "animated" I decided to have Brian use them in a functional manner when I spoke their names.

So I detached the recording devices from the four objects and went low-tech. With three objects placed in front of him, I'd say an object's name and help Brian use it appropriately rather than point to it.

Figure 27 With a little practice, Brian was able to sort different objects into clear bins based on the object placed in front of the bin.

After working like this for a few hours, it became apparent that I should start again with new objects. Brian had been working on pointing to these four objects for over a month. It was too difficult for him to start something new with them.

So I introduced three new objects: a hat (which he would 'put on' when I said "hat"), a book (which he would 'open' when I said "book"), and a ball (which he would 'toss' to me when I said "ball"). I could have made full commands, "put on the hat," "open the book," and "throw the ball" rather than saying nouns, "hat," etc. But I thought all those words might be confusing and I really wanted him to learn the noun. I didn't want him cueing on the wrong word and associating that word with the object.

Brian was quick to pick up the actions for the new objects, and within two hours he was identifying "hat" with 100% accuracy, though he continued to mix up "book" and "ball." Even after repeated work, Brian was unable to learn them, but now he did know two nouns: handkerchief and hat.

Encouraged by our partial success, I decided to introduce three more objects, hoping he could also learn them through functional use. They were: shoes (which he would point to with his foot—it was too much work for him to actually put on

Receptive Skills

Figure 28 An example of a two-step process of receptive labeling. I say the name of the object and Brian had to locate it, use it, and press the recorder which would echo its name.

a shoe), a brush (which he would use to brush his hair), and a truck (which he would push—it was different from the previous one). At first I thought he was learning them, but after repeated work clearly he hadn't. He also hadn't been able to learn book and ball after additional work.

As a result, I decided to back up a step and work on sorting objects by noun. The following occurred to me: even if Brian learned a particular object had a name—for example, a given book was called, 'book'—he might not grasp that other books were also called 'book.' He might not be able to make that generalization. I reasoned that this sorting work might need to precede receptive labeling.

To do this sorting work, I gathered many different books, balls, shoes, trucks, hats, etc., together. None of the objects were identical and there was a wide variety for each noun. For example, there were balls of all sizes and colors.

I put three large, clear bins in front of Brian, each containing a different object. I also put an object in front of each bin (that matched the object in the bin). Then I handed Brian one object at a time, saying its name (*e.g.*, book or ball). He then had to put the object in the correct bin (see Figure 27).

At first, Brian couldn't sort any of these objects. But with a little practice, he was able to sort all of them. This was nice to see. It took him about two weeks to become proficient at sorting these objects.

But even after Brian learned to sort all the objects by noun, he still didn't know their names (except for handkerchief and hat). I needed to find a way to emphasize noun names while Brian sorted the objects. I thought of the recording devices. So I recorded names of the three nouns he was to sort, one per device, and I placed the corresponding recorders in front of each bin. I then made the sorting of nouns into a two-step process: first, I'd say the noun name and hand the object to Brian; then he'd put the object in the appropriate bin, and press the play button on the recorder to echo back the name of the noun.

It just took a few hours for Brian to learn how to do this.

I did a similar two-step process with receptive labeling. I placed a recorder in back of each of the three objects that Brian had to identify with each name recorded on it (see Figure 28). Next I said the noun name to Brian, and he had to locate the object and use it functionally. Then he pressed the play button on the recorder in back of the object, to echo back the noun name. I used the TEACCH pegboard concept so Brian knew when he was finished.

Over the next week, while doing the two-step strategies with sorting and receptive labeling, Brian finally started to learn the names of the nouns.

Receptive Skills

Looking back, three things had to be done for Brian to learn object names receptively: 1. he had to sort objects by noun; 2. use objects functionally; 3. get auditory feedback from the recorders. At the present time, Brian knows seven nouns receptively: handkerchief (a plain, white one), hat (three of these), book (seven), ball (four), brush (one), truck (two) and shoes (four pairs).

• Summary of receptive labeling

The work with musical sounds was a preliminary step for teaching Brian to discriminate between different, nonverbal sounds. Attaching recorders to objects to voice their own names and using the repetition/interruption concept was also helpful in teaching Brian to discriminate between sounds of two different words. Using hand-over-hand prompting helped Brian recognize that the word I spoke was a command—or discriminative stimulus—and cueing with duplicate objects helped him to look at the actual objects. The TEACCH pegboard idea was effective in showing him when he had made a correct response and when he was done with the session. Finally, sorting objects by noun, using them functionally, and getting auditory feedback from recorders were key to Brian's actual success in learning this skill.

More Receptive Labeling Ideas

Since we did experience some success in receptive labeling and noun name recognition, and I felt this area was especially critical, I wanted to intensify our work here. After some thought, I came up with the idea of having specific "noun days" where we emphasized certain nouns.

On noun day all activities are related to a specific subject. For example, on "car day" we do lots of thematic activities and I say the word 'car' many times. All materials unrelated to cars are put away.

Typical car day activities include: spelling car repeatedly on computer and toy alphabet keyboards *(see Chapter Eight, Beginning to Type Independently, pg. 83);* matching car photos and picture symbols; matching the word car to these photos and picture symbols; each time he places a picture, photo or word on the pile, he presses the recorder's play button, programmed to say "car"; and saying the beginning sound of the word car using a computer program (that shows a photo of a car while voicing the word 'car').

Note that all these activities can be done with any noun, just substitute the word, *e.g.,* ball, cup, etc., for car.

Brian also does car-specific activities: pushing cars across a table; putting cars down various tracks; putting a toy person in a larger car and pushing it across the floor; using his communication device to request two car-related activities with the 'do something together' category—using a radio-controlled car and a motorized car racing set.

> *We structured "noun days" in part to introduce Brian to appropriate play skills and to give both of us a much-needed break from our everyday routine. Actually, we often do "noun half-days" since I don't always have enough activities to keep Brian interested for an entire day. Also, we often repeat a noun day several times in a row to give Brian a more complete understanding of it.*

Chapter Six

Receptive Skills

We have other specific noun day activities. For example, on 'ball day' we throw, roll and bounce balls. Brian also uses a lightweight bowling ball to knock down empty plastic soda bottles in the hall. On 'cup day' Brian works on pouring skills and gives pretend drinks to stuffed animals. On 'spoon day' he feeds, stirs and eats with stuffed animals. He also puts away spoons in the cutlery drawer. On 'hat day' Brian puts hats on the heads of his stuffed animals as well as on himself. On 'shoes day' he puts on everyone's shoes and walks around. He also puts the shoes back where they belong. On 'book day' I read to Brian while he turns the pages. He also puts books back on the shelf.

Activities listed above are at his current level of understanding. Other children will be ahead of or behind Brian in performing various skills. When trying this, tailor activities to each child's level of functioning. For example, if a child can't do identical picture matching, there's no point in matching different photos and picture symbols of cars. Matching ten identical pictures (or photos) of the same car would be more appropriate. For a child with more advanced writing skills, draw a picture of a car using step-by-step directions or write out the word car.

Art and music activities featuring the specific noun of the day can also provide fun and productive learning experiences.

I'm happy to say that noun days have been very successful with Brian. He seems to enjoy the activities and the change of pace and has a more complete understanding of each noun we've worked on.

Noun days have been very successful. Brian seems to enjoy the activities and the change of pace.

Chapter Seven

Communication Skills

Beginning to Use a Photo Communication System

Since Brian was older, nonverbal and had few signs, I wanted to find a communication system to use with him. I chose the Picture Exchange Communication System (PECS). PECS is widely used because it works well with so many children. For parents and teachers interested in this subject, but unfamiliar with this system, I recommend reading the PECS Training Manual, by Lori Frost and Andrew Bondy, before continuing with this chapter. In addition, I urge parents and teachers to try the PECS method exactly as it's presented, before trying the ideas here. The majority of children who use the method outlined in the PECS Training Manual become successful communicators. The ideas in this chapter have worked for only one child.

I used the PECS methodology to teach Brian the skill of initiating requests.[9] This was highly successful, as Brian would approach me, spontaneously and independently, to give me a picture symbol. He would even seek me out in another room.

However, Brian was unable to learn the skill of picture discrimination. Although he knew the pictures on his board were useful for "getting good things," he failed to understand that each picture stood for a particular item. He tended to use any picture to represent any of a number of needs and wants.

Initially, I used picture symbols (not photos) on Brian's picture communication board. He seemed to do well using four or five of the symbols, but he was always inconsistent. He never got to the point where I could confidently add pictures to his board. I should add that we started using PECS a few months before he learned picture to picture matching. But even after he could match pictures and objects to photos he was unable to progress with his communication system.

The PECS teaching method helped Brian learn to make requests by giving me a picture symbol.

One day as a test, I watched to see if Brian could match a few objects to their corresponding picture symbols. These were objects that weren't on his communication board: a small, blue-handled pair of scissors; a small, red, toy firetruck; a small, brown plastic horse; and a silver bell. I enlarged the picture symbols of these objects to three-inch squares and colored in the pictures to match the

Communication Skills

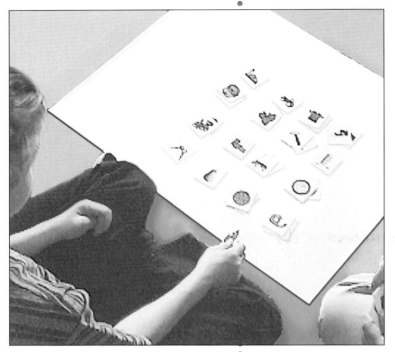

objects. I worked with Brian for several hours a day, for almost a week, doing drills in every way I could think to teach him to match objects to symbols. But after all this work, he would still put the red fire truck on the picture of the scissors (which had the handles colored blue), and the brown horse on the picture of the fire truck (which was colored red), etc. And at this point, he was able to match colors fairly well. I thought coloring in the pictures would be a big help and I thought that the pictures were fairly obvious.

Unfortunately, object to picture symbol work seemed to be going nowhere. But, Brian had proven he could do object to picture matching with a set of objects that had pictures of near-photographic likeness *(see Chapter Five, Object to Photo (Picture) Matching)*. So I decided to take photographs of the four objects mentioned above plus about ten others to see if Brian could match the objects to their photos. When the photos came back, I placed three in front of him and handed him the objects one at a time. He could correctly place the objects without hesitation. We quickly increased to eight photos without any problems. He matched all the objects to their photos accurately. Obviously, photographs were the way to go with his communication board, and picture symbols needed to be put aside for the time being.

I immediately set about taking photos of all the important things in Brian's life, toys, food, etc. I replaced the four picture symbols with the new photos and expected Brian's communication to take off. However, it didn't happen. He chose one photo and used it to express all his wants and needs.

I thought and thought about what was going on. He could easily match the four objects (plus many others) to their photos, yet when he chose a photo on his communication board, it seemed to lose its meaning. In other words, choosing a photo didn't necessarily mean he wanted the object. In addition, he tended to choose one particular photo most of the time.

I decided that Brian needed to master the photo to object "give me" skill. He had to be able to give me the photo that matched the object I was holding, when two or more different photos were placed in front of him. I felt this was the key skill necessary for mastering a picture communication system.[10] It's one of two ways of checking if a child is correctly discriminating between two pictures. I believe the PECS authors didn't intend for this skill to be taught via drill work, since they caution to "...use this method only if you are sure the item being offered is one the student really wants and that the 'distractor' picture is of an item the student does not want."[11] Since I was working intensively on the photo to object "give me" skill, with any and all objects via drills, I was straying from the PECS methodology.

> ***B**rian had to master the photo to object "give me" skill — to be able to give me the photo that matched the object I was holding.*

Chapter Seven

Communication Skills

To work with Brian on the new matching skill, I held one object in my hand, and he had to give me the matching photo from the two or three in front of him. After handing me the correct photo, I'd give him the object for five or ten seconds, retrieve it and start with a new one. If he handed me the wrong photo (*i.e.,* it didn't match the object I held), I wouldn't give him the object. The purpose of these drills was to teach him to recognize the correlation between photo and object.

This matching skill was hard for Brian and he wasn't able to do it right away. While he could perform the skill well with small objects (ones that fit on the photos), with larger ones, he wasn't able to do the skill at all.

It occurred to me that being able to do regular photo to object matching (before attempting the "give me" skill) might make the difference. At the time, Brian was only able to do object to photo matching.

So I began teaching Brian the skill of photo to object matching. We started with simple drills, having two or three objects out, and handing him photos one at a time to place on the correct object. With small objects he could do it easily and with larger, flat ones (*e.g.,* videotapes and books) he learned the skill without too much trouble. However, with larger, 3–D objects he had an hard time. It took many hours of work before he was able to match a photo to a larger, 3–D object (see Figure 29).

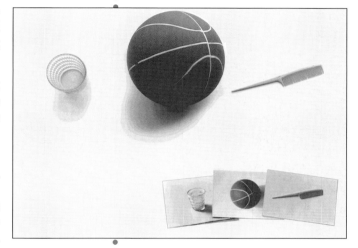

Nonetheless, after having some success with photo to object matching, his performance on the "give me" skill improved. One thing that helped a lot when he was struggling with this skill was to stop working on it and go back to object to photo matching. After a bit of this "refresher course," we'd resume working on the photo to object "give me" skill. Usually, this was enough to get him back on track. If it wasn't, we'd go back to object to photo and photo to object drills.

Because acquiring a picture communication system was so critical to Brian's future progress, we worked on photo to object "give me" drills for many hours. I put aside most other work for a month while concentrating on this. But it paid off. After all this work, he was able to do this skill well with over a dozen photos and objects. And it was easy for him to generalize when I introduced new photos. In addition, his success allowed me to switch from 3 $1/_2$" x 5" photos to wallet-sized reprints. All photos were kept in a loose-leaf notebook. Gradually, as Brian learned to flip through it for photos of objects I was holding, I was able to add to the notebook (see Figure 30).

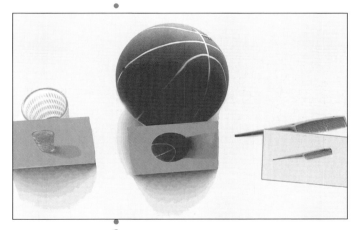

Figure 29 *Photo to object matching.*

Chapter Seven

Communication Skills

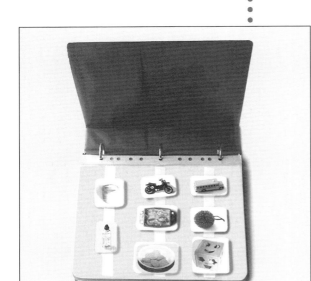

Figure 30 Brian's success at recognizing objects allowed me to put wallet-sized photos in a loose-leaf notebook.

Figure 31 Brian's wallet notebook containing miniature photos that he carries with him at all times.

One thing that helped him locate the photos was making each page a different color. Eventually, Brian was able to switch to a small wallet notebook containing miniature photos which were reduced in size on a color copier. He carried his wallet with him at all times (see Figure 31).

Once Brian mastered the photo to object "give me" skill, he was able to spontaneously select and hand me photos of things he appeared to want—as long as the objects were in view. In other words, when objects were kept in sight—but out of reach—Brian was able to use his communication system well.

However, when objects were not in view, his use of the communication system deteriorated rapidly. When objects were put away, Brian reverted to choosing a single photo to represent all his needs and wants.

It was difficult to keep all objects displayed, but out of reach, since we don't have high shelves in our house. If I ever left the room where objects were displayed, Brian could grab them without bothering to communicate. So the objects had to be hidden.

At first, I posted the 3 $\frac{1}{2}$" x 5" photo originals on the doors where objects were kept to help him remember the hidden items. For example, I put food and drink photos on the refrigerator door. But this didn't help him because objects were spread too far throughout our house.

What helped was putting objects in large, hinged boxes in one room, except for food and drink items, which were kept in the refrigerator. The 3 $\frac{1}{2}$" x 5" photos were posted on these boxes, which were kept locked (see Figure 32). We had one clear box which was especially helpful, since Brian could see the objects even when closed. Eventually, he also learned the contents of the boxes that he couldn't see into. The concept of putting objects in boxes with large pictures to identify the contents is suggested in the PECS Training Manual as a way to help with picture discrimination.[12] However, I had a different goal—to teach object permanence.

Also, I wanted to eliminate the delay between Brian handing me a photo and getting the object. I suspected that during this time lapse, Brian might forget what he requested, thus missing the point of the drill. This could be the reason he was making poor choices when objects were out of sight. So I added an extra, if temporary, step to Brian's communication routine. When he spontaneously brought me a photo of an object hidden in the boxes, I said its name and let him hold on to its photo (rather than handing it to me) while I led him to its box. Then he'd match his photo to the corresponding one posted on the box and I'd repeat its name. Finally, I'd get the object, he'd give me the photo in exchange for it, and I'd say its name a last time.

If Brian gave me a photo of an object that was displayed (*i.e.*, out of its box), I'd just give it to him, rather than going to the box or refrigerator, since in these instances he was choosing the item appropriately.

Communication Skills

I realized that by adding this extra step, Brian might stop seeking me out, instead matching his photos to the large ones on the boxes. But Brian had learned to initiate, via the PECS Training Manual[13] method, and was in the habit of finding me to give me his photos. This continued to be his first choice, even after adding the extra step.

I did various drills to help him find the photos. First, I opened a box to see what object Brian reached for, and had him give me the corresponding photo from his communication notebook. I also held up the other objects in the box and had him give me their photos in exchange for the objects.

When I felt he was familiar with the contents of the box, I closed the lid and pointed to one of the photos. Then in exchange for the object, Brian had to find and give me the corresponding photo from his communication notebook.

If the box had a single large photo posted, Brian figured out immediately what he was supposed to do. But where two or more photos were posted, pointing to a particular photo meant nothing to him. I had to cover the other photos on the box before pointing made sense to him.

In addition, to help Brian make sense of my pointing to photos on the boxes, I worked on his pointing skills. To do this, I placed one or more picture cards in front of him, and encouraged him to point to the picture that I held up and was pointing to.

After a few days of this work, my cueing (pointing to the photos on the boxes) started to become meaningful to him. He became accurate at finding the corresponding photo in his communication notebook.

When I was confident Brian understood the meaning of each large photo on the boxes, I began to cue him by gesturing towards the box and letting him choose the photo of any object inside. Then I gave it to him. This work was done incidentally throughout the day.

Soon after this, Brian began effectively using his communication system. He'd go over to a box, look at the photos on it, find the corresponding one in his communication notebook and bring it to me. Also, he was able to bring me a photo without looking at the boxes, then go over to the appropriate box (by himself or with minimal help) and match his photo (to the one on the box) with no help. This showed me he knew what he was selecting.

Before long—by now Brian was 11—he could work with 27 mini-photos in his wallet communication notebook. I gradually faded the extra step of having him match his photos to the large ones posted on the boxes. He had to bring his photos directly to me or anyone else in the room. However, I didn't fade the use of objects in boxes with the large photos posted on top. They still sit in our living room. Let me say it was truly wonderful that at 11 years of age, Brian finally had an

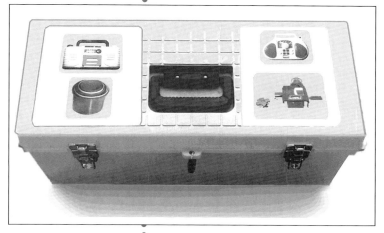

Figure 32 To help Brian communicate to get things he wanted, objects were locked in hinged boxes with photos representing the contents.

It was truly wonderful that at 11 years of age, Brian finally had an effective communication system. And today, he's even a little further ahead with his communication skills.

Chapter Seven

Communication Skills

Figure 33 To help Brian express the fundamental needs of sleep and bathroom, I posted photos of his bed and the bathroom. After three weeks, Brian could spontaneously choose the bed or bathroom photos from his notebook.

effective communication system. And today, he's even a little further ahead with his communication skills.

• Two more successes

Before I continue, I'd like to mention two more successes:

1. It was important that Brian master the ability to express a pair of fundamental needs, bathroom and bed. These needs came up every day, but didn't lend themselves readily to a picture exchange system. To help Brian understand the visual expressions for these needs, I posted a large photo of his bed on his bedroom door and a large photo of the toilet on the bathroom door. I attached the photos with hook and loop fasteners for easy removal (see Figure 33). Every night, before he went to bed, I took the photo of his bed off his door and held it up so he could find the matching photo in his notebook. When he gave me the photo, he could go to bed. I gradually held it further away from him until I could leave it on his bedroom door and simply gesture toward it. That was his prompt to produce it from his wallet when it was time to go to bed. I only did this once a day. I followed a parallel procedure with bathroom needs, when I saw him heading there, the difference being that it was more than once a day. After two weeks, he understood bed and bathroom receptively. After three weeks, he could choose bed and bathroom photos spontaneously, indicating he was tired or needed to use the bathroom.

2. We had an unexpected and wonderful result from using PECS. Once he mastered the use of the 27 photos, Brian was able to understand, receptively, five words for items he commonly requested: blanket, music, video, bathroom, and bed. I was sure he understood them, because when I'd say one, he'd quickly get out his wallet, find the correct photo and hand it to me. As Frost and Bondy report, "children who use 30 to 100 pictures often start to speak while handing over the pictures."[14] Of course, the authors were referring to preschoolers and Brian was 11. This doesn't mean I expected him to start talking, but he clearly learned some words receptively, even if he couldn't use them expressively. And when he switched to the communication device mentioned in the next chapter, he learned an additional five words receptively.

Communication Skills

Excellent Product Alert

Wallet Communication Notebooks
There are a number of different-sized wallets, besides the one I've adapted for Brian's communication system. Several kinds are available through:

Crestwood Company
6625 N. Sidney Pl.
Milwaukee, WI 53209-3259
414-352-5678

Boardmaker© Software
Invaluable for use in designing communication boards. Has three thousand images in color and black and white, all easily accessible through a word-finding and content library. (Note: Boardmaker pictures are seen throughout this book).
Available by calling or writing:

Mayer-Johnson Company
P.O. Box 1579
Solana Beach, CA 92075-1579
619-481-2489

Picture Cue Dictionary
Five interactive software programs to help students perform everyday life skill activities independently. Available from:

Attainment Company, Inc.
P.O. Box 930160
Verona, WI 53593
800-327-4269

Chapter Seven

Communication Skills

Using a Communication Device

A speaking communication device isn't a necessity, but it's certainly nice to have. Using photos or pictures to communicate, either by pointing to them, or exchanging them for desired objects (PECS) is sufficient. In fact, if the pictures are small (made via color-copier or computer) and kept in a wallet, this low-tech system has the advantage of being lightweight, portable and flexible. However, it's likely that in the near future there will be a variety of high-tech communication devices that will share these attributes, while having many benefits these primitive systems could never possess.

I had a few reasons for switching Brian to a speaking device. The first was curiosity; could he do it now that he had a good understanding of the photos? The second was that we happened to have a large speaking device with a grid of 36 squares. The last was that Brian's wallet ripped at the place where I had punched a hole in it. *(Note: it had been attached to his waistband via a retractable chain; use a grommet when punching a hole).*

We had purchased a lower-end-of-the-spectrum speaking device five years earlier to see if Brian could use it to communicate. Despite two years of trying, he never mastered it and eventually we put it away and forgot about it.

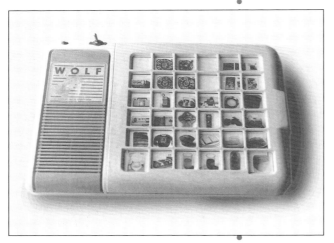

***Figure 34** Brian's WOLF communication device.*

So I took it out of storage and color-copied Brian's 27 photos to the size of the squares on the device. I programmed it to say each word when Brian pressed the photos. At first I had Brian use the device without the raised grid that came with it, but he would just slide his finger all over it going from one photo to another. He needed the raised grid because it separated the photos. But even with the grid, he had a difficult time locating a photo on the device when I held up an object. We worked with the device for a few days, but he didn't seem to get it. (I put out all 27 photos at once; it's possible if I had started with just a few, he might have done much better.)

I concluded that Brian needed to work more on his pointing skills. Since we still had photos posted on the boxes and refrigerator, I tried to use these for pointing to request items. These photos were larger than those on the device, and they were closer to the objects. I put the device away for two weeks while we worked on pointing to the large photos. I presented drills similar to those in the previous chapter: *e.g.,* I held up an object, and Brian had to find and point to its photo to get it. He got this skill quickly.

Once he'd mastered pointing to the large photos, he had no trouble switching to the communication device (see Figure 34). It took about a month for him to use the device well (with me presenting drills similar to those in the previous chapter).

This was great, but the device was large and not very portable. I decided to ask for an Augmentative Communication Evaluation, which is usually paid for by insurance, the school district, or Medicaid. We got one through our school district and Brian was approved for a smaller, hand-held device with a grid of 15 squares. It had four levels of programming for a total of 48 choices.

While it might seem that 48 choices would be too few, my plan was to have them stand for categories, rather than specific items. This way the device would continue to be useable for a long time. To make specific choices, Brian first selected the category on his device, (see Figure 35) then selected from photos in a thin notebook that I carried. That's the subject of the next section.

Using Categories on a Communication Board or Device

Soon after Brian mastered the use of a large communication device he was able to recognize well over 100 photos. He'd generalized this skill and was able to recognize most new photos instantly. However, on the new hand-held speech output device he was to get, only 12 choices were available (it has 15 squares, but three are used to access the other levels). I wanted Brian's communication system to be portable so he could have it with him at all times. And I wanted him to use a wallet notebook or small hand-held device, instead of large, unwieldy ones. Therefore, I wanted to see if he could learn some general categories so he could use a concise main menu in his wallet or on the device, allowing him to access other pages in his notebook or other levels of his speech output device.

I'd set up his wallet the same as the device and would continue to use the notebook when it was unwise to use the device: *e.g.*, when there's a risk of getting it wet or full of sand, etc. In addition to its other uses, the notebook served as a backup communication system (see Figure 36). *(Brian now uses a speaking communication device, but in this chapter I refer to the notebook because that's how he learned these skills.)*

The first two categories I wanted Brian to learn were eat and drink. To do this, I replaced food and drink photos in his wallet with picture symbols which went on the first page (main menu). When he handed me an eat or drink symbol, I produced a set of photos to choose from (usually by pointing, or as pictures to be exchanged). The same photos were posted on the refrigerator. Later, I arranged photos in a thin notebook I carried. Photos included: a page of breakfast choices; a page of lunch choices; a page of snack choices; a page for drinks at home; two pages for choices at restaurants we commonly go to; and a page for drinks at a shopping mall. So depending on the circumstances – *e.g.*, time of day, where we are, etc. – when Brian gave me an eat or drink picture, I gave him appropriate choices. Sometimes there was only one food or drink choice available, like water, and if he handed me the drink symbol at that point, I just gave him water. I didn't bother to display a choice of photos.

> *To get approved for a device, the child must be able to demonstrate independent, functional use with it. If a parent is trying to get a device through the evaluation process, but the child doesn't have the skills to use it independently, then it's probably best not to waste the time and money, because it's not likely to be approved. Five years earlier, we took Brian for the same evaluation and weren't approved because he couldn't use any of the devices independently. It was at that evaluation that I saw the WOLF device and decided to buy it to see if Brian could eventually use it. We paid for it.*

Figure 35 *Brian's hand-held communication device, the Vocal Assistant.*

Communication Skills

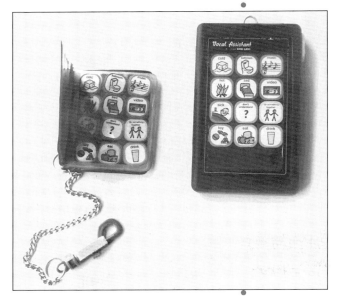

Figure 36 Brian's wallet notebook and the Vocal Assistant device.

Getting Brian to use picture symbols was difficult, almost like teaching him a new language. It took him several months to crack the code, and he was frustrated during this time, since we had replaced the communication system he was comfortable with. When he learned a communication system and I'd change it, it was upsetting to him. But I felt being able to categorize and use a main menu page was a valuable skill to learn. It would eventually lead us to the best and most flexible system available to him as a person with no speech and few signs. (Unless someday he started to type independently.) And if he just wasn't able to learn it, we could always go back to an all-photo system.

To teach Brian the eat and drink symbols, I posted copies on the refrigerator next to the large photos. When he was hungry, I'd have him point to the food photo he wanted and then help him find the picture symbol for eat, which was next to the group of food photos. Then I'd have him find the matching picture symbol for eat in his wallet notebook. Later, he'd notice the eat symbol on the refrigerator, and immediately hand me his symbol, after which I would ask him to show me (by pointing) what he wanted to eat. But it would be several months more before Brian would spontaneously bring me pictures to request food or drink, without first looking at the picture symbols on the refrigerator.

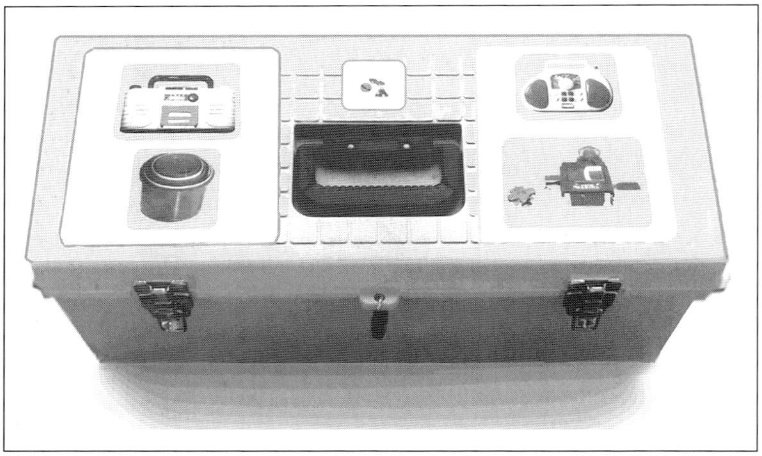

Fortunately, some picture symbols took Brian a little less time to understand. I introduced three picture symbols of leisure activities Brian enjoys: listening to music, watching a video and playing with toys in the living room. These activities were represented by music, video and toy picture symbols. To get the idea of these activities across to Brian I placed picture symbols in the following locations: the music symbol on the corner of the large music photo (on the music cabinet); the video symbol on the corner of the video photo (on the video cabinet); the toy symbol on each of the two boxes in the living room that held the toys (see Figure 37). When Brian indicated wanting one of these items (by pointing to the photos), I showed him the picture symbol (on the music cabinet, video cabinet or toy box) and had him find and give me the corresponding small picture symbol from his wallet notebook. Within two months Brian was correctly and spontaneously using these three picture symbols to request these items.

Figure 37 One of the boxes holding toys with a small toy symbol.

I recently started to teach a category I call "do something together." It's for activities Brian enjoys, but can't do without close supervision, for example: playing outside, using the computer, and playing with fragile toys. I put a large photo of each activity on a piece of poster board, and in the upper left corner, a picture symbol representing the category (two people holding hands—see Figure 38). I put it up in

Chapter Seven

Communication Skills

the hall. He has requested a number of these activities by pointing to the photos and finding the matching symbol in his wallet notebook. He still has to look at the picture on the poster board before making the requests, as he doesn't know the meaning of its symbol yet (see Figure 39).

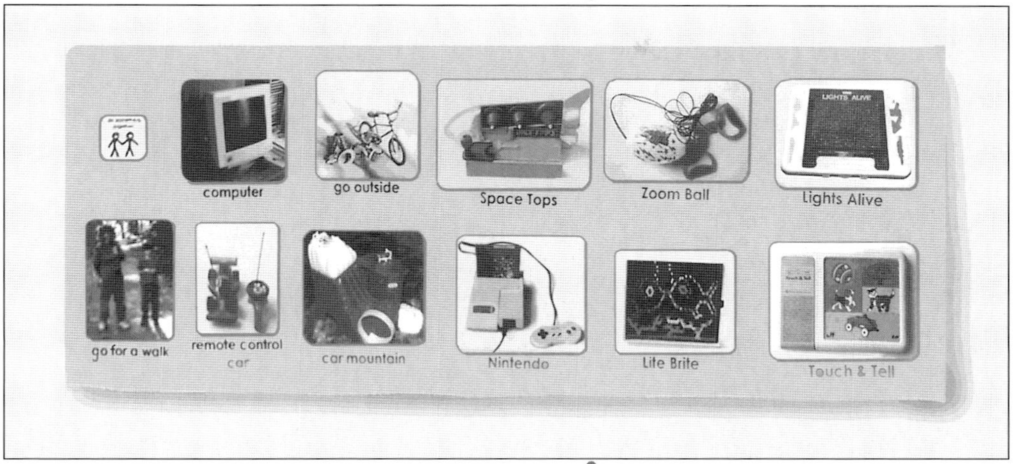

Two other important categories were bed and bathroom. Brian could already use bed and bathroom photos to express his needs. While I could have left these photos on the main menu, other categories were represented by picture symbols. So I introduced picture symbols for them as well. To help Brian learn the symbols for bed and bathroom, I placed the bed symbol on the corner of the large bed photo (on his bedroom door) and the bathroom symbol on the corner of the bathroom photo (on the frame of the bathroom door—see Figures 40–41). I repeated the work described in *Chapter Seven, Beginning to Use a Photo Communication System,* for teaching these two concepts. But this time we used picture symbols rather than photos. Brian is just starting to use these picture symbols spontaneously and appropriately.

Figure 38 The "do something together" activities posted in the hallway.

In addition, there were two new categories I wanted Brian to learn, "cold" and "hot." Brian isn't happy when he's too hot or cold. I placed a picture symbol for cold near the photos on the box (in the living room) that contains a blanket and sweatshirt. Brian learned this one quickly and can hand me his small cold symbol and point to a large photo to request a blanket or sweatshirt. I haven't started to teach the hot symbol yet, but Brian's choices will be: a t-shirt, a pair of shorts, and an ice cube (see Figure 42).

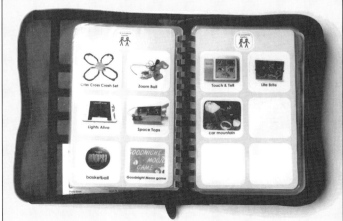

Brian's doctor suggested the next category, "I feel sick." Brian was seeing her because of an injured toe and the doctor felt it was important for him to communicate when he didn't feel well. This is an extremely abstract concept for Brian to communicate, more so than cold, hot, bathroom or bed. But it's very important. So I placed a picture symbol for "sick" on the main menu of his notebook. I also made a copy of the symbol so I could hold it up at appropriate times until he found his matching symbol. He doesn't know how to use this symbol yet, but here's how I intend to teach the concept: when Brian has an injury and I change the dressing, I will hold up my picture symbol of sick to cue him to select his. When he's sneezed from a cold and has been cleaned up, I will cue him to select sick by holding up my

Figure 39 Some of the "do something together" activities in the thin notebook.

Chapter Seven

Communication Skills

Figures 40-41 *To help Brian learn the symbols for bed and bathroom, I placed the bed symbol on the corner of the large photos on the bedroom and bathroom doors.*

symbol. I'll also do this after he has been coughing or has thrown up. It may take years for him to learn the meaning of this symbol, but it's an important one for him to acquire.

Another category I am starting to teach is, "this work is too difficult." It's important for Brian, because he's frequently aggressive when he can't figure out the correct answer during work. So when I notice he's making incorrect responses and starting to get upset—but has yet to become aggressive—I hold up a copy of the "don't understand" picture symbol. Then he must find a copy of the symbol in his notebook to hand to me. At that point I'm aware he's having a hard time and offer easier work.

There's several categories that are not on Brian's main menu but may be of interest to others: 'I want to access a keyboard' (for those who can communicate by typing); 'I want to access a social conversation page,' with greetings like, "Hi, how are you?" (for those who understand this idea); 'yes/no' (for those who grasp this concept). Some children will be able to handle these categories while others will not.

Summary

Brian's main menu contains the following categories: everyday needs, which include eat, drink, bathroom, bed; being uncomfortable, which include hot, cold, sick; leisure activities he enjoys independently, which include music, video, toy; a leisure activity he can't do independently, "do something together"; and a work-related category, "this work is too difficult."

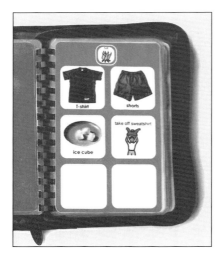

Figure 42 *Brian's choices to communicate "hot."*

Communication Skills

> ### *Excellent Product Alert*
>
> More than half of the food photos in Brian's communication notebook come from the *Picture This* CD-ROM. It contains over 2,400 high-resolution photo images that can be used for making flash cards, lotto boards and communication boards. Though I've only used these images for some of Brian's communication choices, they can also be used for teaching beginning matching skills *(Chapter Five)*, because with a computer it's easy to print multiple copies of the same image. In addition, this CD-ROM can be used to create the photos for object to photo matching *(Chapter Five)*.

Picture This CD-ROM
Picture This has photo images of a number of items like clothespins, paper clips, pencils, etc., which you can match to objects by locating similar items around the house or school. It is available from:

Silver Lining Multimedia, Inc.
P.O. Box 2201
Poughkeepsie, NY 12601
914-462-8714
www.silverliningmm.com

Assistive Technology Devices
There are literally hundreds of different assistive technology devices available, and more new ones every day it seems. Here are some lower end of the spectrum devices. Each has its own special features and while some do many things and are expensive, others are simple with few features and are relatively inexpensive. Your choice depends on your need and budget. The following products – Vocal Assistant, WOLF, YAKBAK 2 – have proven track records:

Vocal Assistant
Is manufactured by GMR Labs and can be purchased through a number of distributors, including:

Luminaud, Inc.
8688 Tyler Blvd.
Mentor, OH 44060
800-255-3408

Communication Skills

WOLF
You can purchase WOLF, or receive a catalog from:

Wayne RESA ADAMLAB
33500 Van Born Rd.
Wayne, MI 48184
734-334-1415

YAKBAK 2
A single message recording toy that I use extensively. It's cheap and durable and can be purchased from:

YES! Entertainment Corporation
3875 Hopyard Rd.
Pleasanton, CA 94588
800-222-9376

Attainment Talkers
Fifteen Talker and Five Talker devices are available from:

Attainment Company
P.O. Box 930160
Verona, WI 53593
800-327-4269

Chapter Eight

Academic Skills

Reading Ideas

When Brian was five, the idea became widespread that children with autism might understand far more than we had realized. Because of this, I started to hope that Brian was intelligent. I began reading to him from age-appropriate books for short periods of time, 10-20 minutes, almost every day. I continue to do this.

I read two types of books to Brian: those with academic content and storybooks appropriate for children his age.

When we read, we sit together on the couch. For a long time, he wouldn't sit still, and got up frequently. Each time this happened, I stopped reading, retrieved him, and continued reading. Gradually, over several months, he learned to stay seated. Sometimes, he was noisy. Again, I stopped reading, said "shhh," and waited until he was quiet before continuing to read.

When Brian was finally able to sit quietly, the reading sessions went well. He has always seemed to enjoy it, as do I. Reading is one of the more relaxing parts of his program, but realistically I have no idea how much he understands.

Once Brian learned to sit quietly, our reading sessions became enjoyable for both of us.

Beginning to Type Independently

Once it occurred to me that Brian might be intelligent, I began to work on supported typing, hoping one day he'd be independent. We worked hard on it for a long time, but I've never been able to totally remove my support, nor tell if I was influencing him or not. I thought I could break down the skill of typing into small parts and have him work at it from the bottom up. If he was intelligent, and had enough low-level typing skills, I hoped he might someday be able to generalize them to type independently.

As a result of our hard work, Brian can type words independently when he sees them spelled out. However, he's a long way from being able to type communicatively. What he's doing is matching letters in sequence. This doesn't prove he can read, but in related areas he's starting to match words to pictures and photos (and pictures to photos), so all of this typing work may eventually be worthwhile.

Academic Skills

To learn to copy words using a keyboard device, Brian had to learn three skills:

1. letter to letter matching;
2. matching letters in sequence;
3. using a keyboard device to type the letter sequence.

• Letter to Letter Matching

A few years before Brian learned to match most of the letters in the alphabet. But nothing I tried at the time seemed to help him get the remaining letters. Eventually, I changed the materials we were using. About seven months ago, I bought a set of white magnetic squares, each with a single lowercase letter (or number) printed in blue. Brian was immediately able to use these to match all of the letters (and numbers). I would place several magnetic letters on the (magnet) board and hand him a letter. He was able to place his letter on top of its match.

Once he could match letters, I wanted to see if he could copy words I spelled with the magnetic letters. This was quite a different skill from matching single letters (placing them on identical letters). We copied words by placing them on the board, and putting out several letters for Brian to choose from. He was to match his letter to the 'leftmost' letter in the word on the board. He couldn't just grab any letter and then see where it went. He had to scan his choices and select the correct letter. A good way to teach this skill is to start the child matching the single letter word "a."

Next, introduce two letters to choose from, *e.g.,* "a" and "t." Place the "a" directly above the choice "a" and ask him to match it (see Figure 43). When he can do it, move the "a" halfway between (and above) the "a" and "t" choices and again ask him to match the "a". If he starts to grab the "t," quickly move the "a" directly above the choice "a" again. When he can do this correctly, gradually add more letters for choices and have him match other letters besides "a." Always correct wrong responses by quickly moving the top letter to above its corresponding choice letter and do it before he picks up the wrong letter. When he can handle three or four letters, gradually move the top one away from the choice letters until he can match it at 6–8 inches distance (see Figure 43).

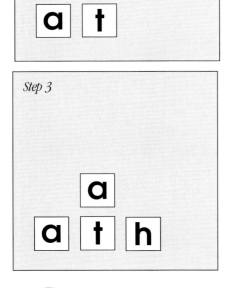

Figure 43 *Matching letters in words: Step 1—put the letter the student is to find directly over the correct choice; student will select the lower "a" and place it on top of the higher "a". Step 2—move the letter in between the two choices. Step 3—put out additional letters to choose from.*

Academic Skills

• Matching Letters in Sequence

To teach Brian to copy words of two or more letters, I placed a short word on the board, and put out the same letters that were in the word as choices, but in mixed order. Since I used magnetic letters, I could dangle them on the edge of the board making it easy for Brian to pick them up.

At first I had Brian place his letters on top of those in the word. This didn't work. Brian appeared to get lost in the word, forgetting which letters he already put down. Another approach was to put his word one or more inches below the word I put out. This was too difficult. Finally, I had him place his letters below the letters in the word, with each one touching its match. He quickly figured this out.

The first words Brian matched were "a," "at," and "hat." I soon added a "c" and "r" so he could spell "cat" and "car." Mostly, we spelled nouns by displaying a picture of the noun above the word he was copying. Next I introduced "s" so he could spell "star." Then "o" and "e" for "shoe." At this point, I tried some longer words which used only these letters, like "teacher," "horse," "store" and "carrot." He had no trouble with these, and had apparently generalized the skill very quickly.

***Figure 43** (Cont.) Matching letters in words: Step 4—move the letter to be matched further away from the choices. Step 5—try having the student match other letters. Step 6—change the order of the choice letters. Step 7-9—match letters to a three letter word; have student place letters (touching) directly underneath the letters in left to right order.*

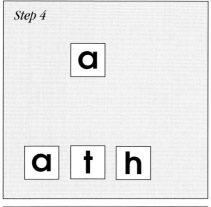

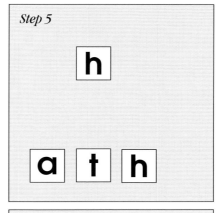

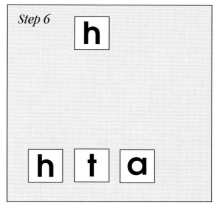

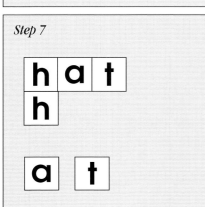

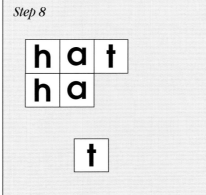

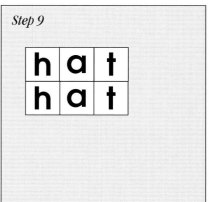

Academic Skills

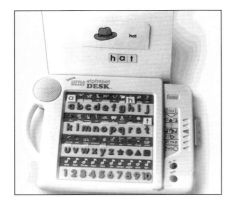

Figure 44 *Using a device to spell the word "hat".*

• Using a Keyboard Device

The next step was to transfer our success to use of a keyboard device. Fortunately, we had a preschool toy that functioned as a keyboard. It had raised lowercase letters with a similar font, size and color to the magnetic letters Brian was using. When you pressed a letter on this device, it would say its name. This was helpful auditory feedback, because while most keyboards will display a letter you typed, they won't say its name. On the other hand, the device had no display feature, so I used the magnet board as the display, showing the word (and its picture) that Brian was to copy. As he typed each letter, I placed a matching magnetic letter directly under the corresponding letter in the word (touching it). This was extremely effective for helping him keep his place in the word as he typed.

I hoped the letters on the device were similar enough to the magnetic ones so he'd have no trouble typing the words. However, he couldn't do it at all. Perhaps the letters on the device looked too different from the magnetic ones. Also, it's likely 26 letters were too many to choose from. I tried placing the magnetic letters "h," "a" and "t" just above their corresponding letters on the device. This narrowed the field to three choices. I spelled "hat" on the magnet board and held up a picture of a hat just above the word. I helped Brian find the "h" by holding a magnetic "h" near the one on the device. Then I helped him slide his finger down to press the "h" on the device just under the magnetic letter. After he pressed it, the device said "h" and I put a magnetic "h" directly under the "h" in "hat" on the magnet board. We did the same for "a" and "t" (see Figure 44). He quickly figured out how to find the letters on the device in correct sequence. After one day, I was able to put more letters on the device. I added "c" and "r" above their corresponding letters on the device. Since there wasn't enough room to fit all the magnetic letters on the device, I printed out a smaller set of letters (using my computer) in a similar font and color to the magnetic ones. Then I cut these letters out, laminated them, and as Brian was able to handle new ones, attached them with hook and loop fasteners to the device.

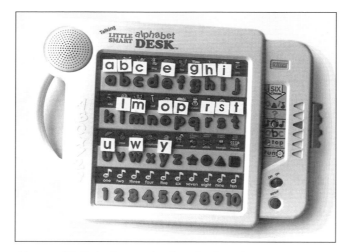

Figure 45 *Brian's preschool toy keyboard as it is now.*

Academic Skills

When "c" and "r" were added, Brian had tremendous confusion between the "t" and "r" on the device, though he had no problem matching them on the magnet board. By backtracking and doing work on the magnet board, we got this straightened out, but it was at least two weeks before I could add another letter. I added letters in the order mentioned above, plus additional ones. The only other problem Brian had was confusing the "a" and "p." Because of this, I was afraid to add the "b," thinking he might be dyslexic, but he had no trouble with it at all (I've yet to try "d"). Brian now chooses from 17 letters on this device, spelling words of any length using these letters (see Figure 45).

His typing is quick and accurate. In the next few months, I hope he can handle all 26 letters. Also, I've started to fade putting up each letter on the magnet board as he types. He's now able to type a number of words if I simply point to the letter he's about to type. On several words, Brian doesn't need me to point at all. He can keep his place without my help. And he types one word, "hat," from looking at its picture, without the word being displayed. I'm also trying to get him to copy a word printed in black rather than blue. Eventually I'll have him copy words with slightly different fonts and font sizes.

I also wanted Brian to learn the standard QWERTY keyboard on a computer. I didn't use magnetic letters for this, since there's no space above each letter on the keyboard for them. And it's not a good idea to use magnets near a computer. Instead I printed out the alphabet in black capital letters with a similar font to those on our keyboard, only slightly larger. I cut out three, H," "A," and "T" and attached them to those keys with double stick tape. This helped single out the three keys from the rest of the keyboard. Printing letters on colored paper would've highlighted them even more, but Brian recognized them without a problem.

Next, I wrote "HAT" on the computer screen (with a similar font and size as the keys) and had Brian type it directly beneath my word. This was too difficult. I cued him by holding up paper copies of the letters above the appropriate keys. With this help, he could type the word, but wasn't able to link the word on the computer screen with keys on the keyboard. The problem was that the computer's response to his pressing a key was instantaneous. He would look at the keyboard to find a letter (this was good) but he couldn't see the computer's response (to pressing the key) because he couldn't look at the keyboard and computer screen at the same time. This made it difficult for him to make the connection between pressing a key and the letter appearing on the computer screen. While Brian was able to use a mouse (*see Chapter Eleven, Beginning to Use a Computer*), it could be used without him actually looking at it; he only needed to focus on the computer screen.

Excellent Product Alert

Fun With Letters

The magnetic letters we used were helpful and durable. It's called the Fun-With-Letters Magnet Set. They can be purchased at many retail stores or from:

Dowling Magnets
P.O. Box 1829
Sonoma, CA 95476
800-624-6381

Figure 46 *The computer keyboard, held on its side under the computer screen; large letters spell "hat" on the screen and paper letters attached to the "h," "a," "t," keys.*

Chapter Eight

Academic Skills

To get Brian to understand the results of his keystrokes, I held the keyboard on its side, in line with the computer screen and beneath it. And I changed the font size of the letters to very large, so when Brian pressed a key he could see the result. After a few days I was able to move the keyboard back to its original position. At this point, Brian could type a letter and see it appear on the computer screen (see Figure 46). To help him keep his place and to know what he had typed, I said each letter as he typed it and pointed to the next one he was to type. I gradually shrunk the size of letters displayed on the screen.

Figure 47 *The computer keyboard as it is now, with Brian recognizing 11 letters.*

After much work with single letters Brian could type a few three letter words if I put several spaces between letters in the model word on the computer screen. When he used the computer keyboard, he had a more difficult time keeping his place in the word than when using the alphabet toy keyboard with the magnetic board. When he loses his place in a word on the computer, he can never find it again so I just have him start over. Because the computer keyboard has been more difficult for Brian, I've labeled only 11 letters on it (see Figure 47).

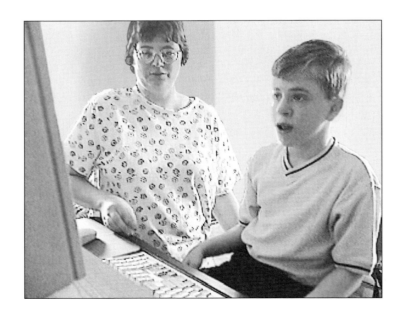

Chapter Eight

Chapter Nine

Fine Motor Skills

Writing Ideas

It took two and a half years of work for Brian to independently copy a circle and horizontal and vertical lines.

During this time, I tried a number of writing "activities" with him, although he hated writing so much that "battles" might be a better word. He gripped the thick marker fiercely and frequently screamed during these sessions. Because we both ended up with our hands covered with marker, I made sure we used washable brands. This clearly was an area where I should have broken down the skill sooner to avoid so much frustration, but I didn't come up with anything helpful until the beginning of the third year of his program.

Initially, during the first year of his program, I tried to have him write two letters or numbers a day. I did this hand-over-hand, trying to get him to write as independently as possible. Soon I added a second activity; tracing horizontal and vertical lines over the ones I drew.

Brian disliked both of these activities, but not knowing what else to do, we continued to work on them almost every day for a year. I wouldn't let him finish a session until he produced two letters and one shape at least once and "nicely." By nicely, I mean to the best of his ability with a normal, relaxed grip on the marker and without screaming or crying. It wasn't fun.

After a year, he still needed supports to write the letters and numbers. He improved at drawing the horizontal and vertical lines, but wasn't independent. He still had no fondness for writing.

Another year passed and Brian needed less support to write letters and numbers, but he still couldn't independently draw any simple shapes.

At the beginning of the third year of writing work, I decided to forget about having Brian write letters and to focus on his independently drawing circles and horizontal and vertical lines. I thought and thought about how to achieve this. I knew from our previous matching work that repetition would be helpful. I also knew he couldn't draw even the simplest of shapes without some support. So I needed a concrete way to fade my support. Also, I wanted this work to be done on a wipe-off board, rather than paper.

After three years of trying to write letters and numbers, we focused on independently drawing circles and lines.

Fine Motor Skills

I came up with a set of stencils, cut out of clear, legal-size sheet protectors that I attached with small pieces of hook and loop fasteners to a large, 18" x 24" wipe-off board. By using stencils, Brian could rely on them rather than on my physical support. Because I used legal-size sheet protectors for the stencils, I could fit three copies of a given shape onto a sheet, giving him some repetition for each shape. I made these shapes large, because his fine motor control wasn't that great. I used clear sheet protectors for the stencils because you can erase wipe-off markers from them. Since Brian often jumped the boundaries and wrote on the stencil, it was nice to have a material that cleaned easily.

The vertical line stencil looked like this:

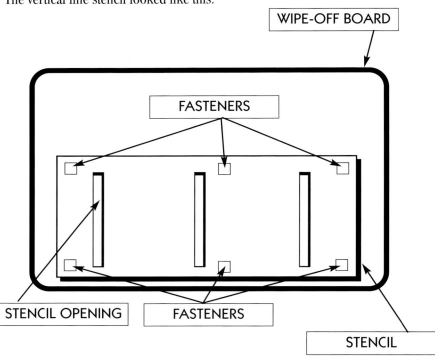

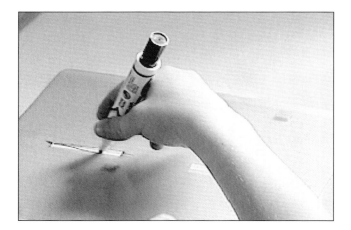

Chapter Nine

An amazing transformation started to happen after using the stencils a few times. Brian started to like writing and was happy during the writing sessions. He took to the stencils like a duck to water. Within a few weeks, he could use the stencils independently for all shapes as long as I initially helped him place the marker within the stencil opening. Within a few weeks, he didn't need help placing his marker. In other words, when using stencils, he could write the shapes without support from me.

The next step was to eliminate stencil use. I wrote the stencil outlines on the wipe-off board to see if he could stay within the lines. The vertical stencil outlines looked like this:

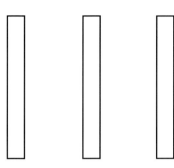

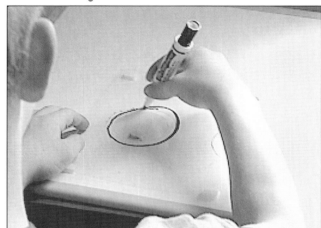

He could do them! It was a major leap forward. I no longer had to use the actual stencils, as long as I drew the stencil shape on the wipe-off board.

Two weeks later, I tried drawing dotted lines instead of outlined stencil shapes:

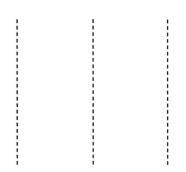

He could do this, too! Soon, he was able to make a few of the shapes independently, while he still relied on tracing dotted lines for the others.

The next step was to learn to copy the shapes I drew. At this point, he could draw some of the easy shapes independently, but couldn't copy them after I drew them.

For several weeks Brian and I worked on copying. We didn't do anything special except hand-over-hand corrections, until he produced the correct shape. I used the

Fine Motor Skills

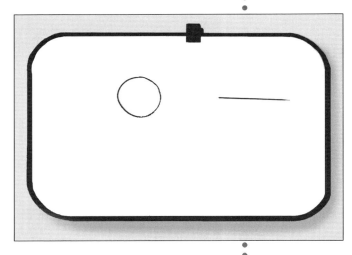

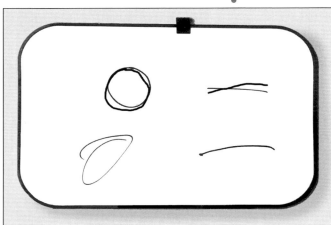

Figures 48 and 49 *So that Brian could not just copy my hand motion, I drew two shapes. The last motion he saw was the wrong shape for the shape he was to copy first.*

TEACCH pegboard idea so he'd know how many shapes he needed to draw. After three weeks, Brian understood copying.

But then I realized Brian was relying on seeing the motion of my hand in order to draw the shape. If he just saw the shape, he wasn't able to copy it at all. To help him get a feel for the direction he'd need to move his hand in, I had him trace the shape I'd drawn before he drew his. It worked. When he first traced the shape before copying it, he was able to independently copy shapes without needing to see my hand motion. The only problem was keeping his eyes covered while I drew shapes so he didn't see the motion of my hand. Instead of turning him away or covering his eyes, I drew two (different) shapes and let him look. This way, the last motion he saw would be the wrong one for the shape he needed to copy first. This kept him from copying my hand motion (see Figures 48 and 49).

Next I had him copy the shapes without first tracing them. I'd let him start to trace the shape I drew, and then interrupt him to see if he could remember the motion and draw the shape himself. It took a long time for him to do, but eventually he got it. A month later, he was able to see a shape (horizontal and vertical line, circle and cross) and copy it without tracing or seeing my hand motion (see Figure 50).

To move toward drawing letters, I first experimented to see if Brian could trace diagonal lines up and down. He could, so I had him trace (not copy) two, and then three of these (horizontal and vertical lines, circle, cross, diagonal lines up and down) on the wipe off board. For example, with dotted lines I drew two circles on the wipe-off board. Then Brian traced over the dotted lines, starting with the leftmost circle first. Or I drew a cross and a vertical line, etc. At first, I drew these shapes far apart on the board, but gradually moved them closer until they were nearly touching. Sometimes I drew one shape over another, and he'd have to first trace the top shape, followed by the bottom one. After he could trace two shapes, I added a third, sometimes having the three arranged horizontally, sometimes vertically. When he could handle these, I decided he was ready to trace letter shapes. And this is where he's at now: able to trace (not copy) many of the letters, upper- and lowercase (see Figure 51).

Note: make sure the correct stroke order is used when drawing shapes and letters. In the beginning, I taught Brian to draw a circle the wrong direction, and he had to re-learn it the correct way, wasting a great deal of time.

Chapter Nine

Fine Motor Skills

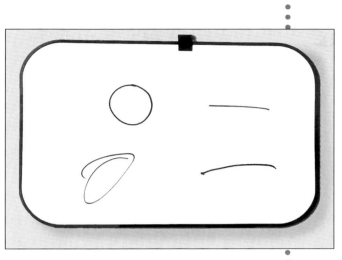

Figure 50 Brian can now see a shape and copy it without tracing or seeing my hand motion.

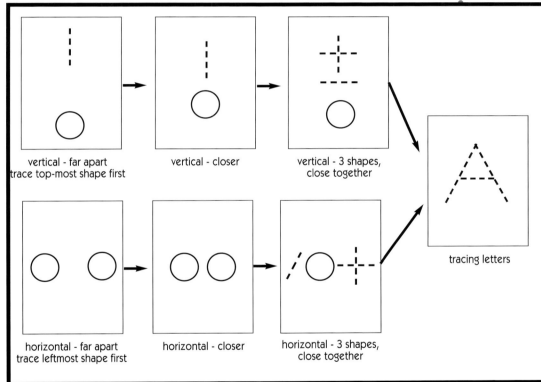

Figure 51 Tracing over these shapes, Brian is now able to trace letters.

Summary

The steps involved in copying shapes were:

- drawing within stencil boundaries (with multiple copies of same stencil shape)
- drawing within (drawn) stencil shapes; tracing dotted line shapes
- tracing sample shape and then copying it
- starting to trace sample shape (without completing it) and then copying it
- copying the sample shape just from looking at it.

Chapter Nine

Fine Motor Skills

Small Model Work

I noticed Brian was far more interested in putting together pieces from toy model kits than he was in baby pop-beads, offered to him at various times from therapists. In keeping with my belief that Brian was intelligent, I decided it would be good for him to work with some age-appropriate fine motor materials, even though the manipulation of these items was far beyond him.

Initially, I chose a nuts and bolts type model kit which used all plastic pieces, and one consisting of plastic rods and connectors in various colors. Brian worked with these kits for a few minutes each day. With each he'd work on starting, continuing or completing a small model from the directions provided. He'd add five or six pieces to a model at each work session, since doing more caused frustration. When a model was completed, he was interested in the finished product and was pleased with himself.

In the beginning, I used total hand-over-hand support, but his dexterity improved with daily practice over a period of several months.

With all small model work, the order of skills—the skill level—he needed to learn was as follows:

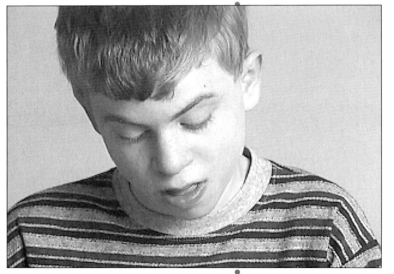

0. Work is done completely hand-over-hand.
1. I hold the model firmly on the table, and line up the next piece to be added, and he attaches the new piece using his right hand.
2. He holds the model firmly on the table with his left hand, and I line up the next piece to be added, while he attaches the new piece using his right hand.
3. He holds the model off the table in his left hand, and with me lining up the next piece to be added, he attaches the new piece using his right hand.
4. He holds the model off the table in his left hand, and lines up the next piece to be added (after I show him where it goes), and he attaches the new piece using his right hand.
5. He holds the model off the table in his left hand, and lines up the next piece to be added (after looking at the schematic instruction for the model), and attaches the new piece using his right hand. In other words, he looks at the directions, figures out where the next piece goes, and puts it on correctly all by himself!

Fine Motor Skills

With the nuts and bolts model kit, Brian performs at varying levels depending on the type of piece he's putting in. For example, he's at level 3 putting screws in holes, because he can do this while holding the model in his left hand—but I can't just point to the hole, I need to line the screw up right next to the hole where it goes. Sometimes he's at level 3 threading nuts onto screws, where he can hold the model in his left hand—but sometimes he's only at level 1, because the nuts can be in awkward places and I have to help hold the model myself. He can usually turn the screwdriver until the nuts are tight while he supports the model in his left hand (level 3)—but I need to attach the screwdriver onto the screw (level 0, he can't do this at all).

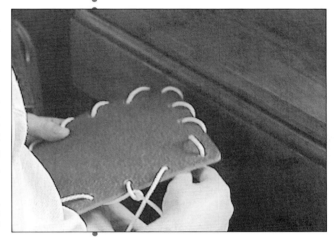

With the rods and connectors model kit, all the pieces are similar, so there aren't many different skills to be learned. Brian learned how to press two pieces together flat on the table using his right index finger within a few weeks (level 1). Yet it took at least six or eight more months before he was able to progress to levels 2 and 3, where he could squeeze two pieces together between his right thumb and forefinger (up off the table).

Getting to level 4 (lining up the pieces) was also tricky. Every time I tried to show him how to line them up he'd look away and wait for me to do it. He did it every time, so it was impossible to show him what to do.

Three things helped him learn this skill:

1. going back to working flat on the table
2. not letting him leave the work area until he had put two pieces together independently
3. and the following idea which I used to catch his attention: lining up the pieces and holding them until he was about to squeeze them together, when he'd briefly look at them. At this point, I'd quickly move the top piece away and hand it to him, saying, "You have to do this." We'd do this twenty times before he'd look at what he was doing, and successfully line them up and put them together. Now Brian is working at level 5. He's matching pieces to their corresponding images following the directions for a few easy models. I cover all but the image of from 1-3 pieces and Brian's able to correctly match and put together these small models.

After working this way every day for about a month, he was able to line up the pieces and put them together, both on and off the table (level 4), completely by himself.

Brian is now matching pieces to their corresponding images and following the directions for a few easy models.

Chapter Nine

Fine Motor Skills

In addition to the two types of kits mentioned above, I've found two others that have interested him. One is a kit for constructing gear-based models using relatively large plastic pieces, and the other is for making battery-operated moving vehicles. Brian's made progress with the manipulation of these materials. He's at level 2 and 3 with most of the different kinds of pieces in these kits.

It's too much to work on each of these model kits every day, so we work on one a day for longer periods of time. Brian is usually able to add 15-20 model pieces per session. His progress would be faster if I worked on each one every day. But, since other skills take precedence, mastery of fine motor model work isn't a high priority. It's like a treat for him, something a little more fun than most of his other work.

In summary, if a child shows no interest in this type of work, is destructive with the materials, or puts them in his mouth, then put this idea on hold for a while and try it again when the child is a little older.

Fine Motor Skills

> ### *Excellent Product Alert*
> The following companies carry products I've found useful when Brian and I do our small model work. Bear in mind that companies change hands, go out of business, etc., over time, making these addresses and phone numbers subject to change. In addition, and perhaps more importantly, these products are available at most large retail toy stores. Or you can call or write the company to request a catalog of their products.

Rod and Connector Model Kits
The company that makes the rods and connectors mentioned in Chapter Nine carry about 50 model kits using these materials as assembly devices. This is a construction toy, available through:

K'NEX
P.O. Box 700
Hatfield, PA 19440-0700
800-543-5639

Erector Set, Jr.
This is the model kit using nuts and bolts referenced in Chapter Nine. This product is like the rod and connector kits or Legos, a construction toy, but is only available through retail stores. However, if you need replacement parts, contact:

Irwin Toy Ltd.
43 Hanna Ave.
Toronto, ON
Canada M6K 1X6
800-347-9313

Duplo-Toolo
The Duplo-Toolo is one of a number of building block set designed by Legos for younger children that can be used in similar tasks as the "kit for constructing vehicles" described in Chapter Nine. Although the Toolo is no longer sold by Legos, there are a number of Duplo sets of varying size that are appropriate for this task. For a catalog, or replacement parts, contact:

Chapter Nine

Fine Motor Skills

Legos Systems
555 Taylor Rd.
Enfield, CT 06082
800-243-4870

Capsela

The Capsela is a motorized model building kit, discussed in Chapter Nine, and is available in most toy stores, or by contacting its manufacturer in England:

VTECH Electronics, Ltd.
3a Colwell Dr.
Abingdon Business Park
Abingdon, Oxon OX14 1AU
United Kingdom

98 Chapter Nine

Chapter Ten

Large Motor Skills

Age-Appropriate Large Motor Skills for Self-Esteem

Many ideas in this chapter are only appropriate for children 5 years or older.

In addition to age-appropriate fine motor skills, we worked on age-appropriate large motor skills, despite the fact that Brian wasn't close to being able to do them. I want to stress that point: initially, Brian was totally unable to do these skills. Unlike middle- and high-functioning children with autism, by the time he was eight, Brian had moderate to severe delays in performing large motor skills.

As with fine motor skills, I worked with Brian on large motor skills a little each day, when the weather was nice. Some activities we did include: riding a bicycle with training wheels; in-line skating; playing catch using mitts which "grip" the ball; playing catch with baseball and glove (it took two months of Sensory Toleration work before Brian was able to wear a mitt); and using a hockey stick to hit a ball through a goal. Other activities I didn't do (but could have) included: throwing a basketball through a hoop, jumping rope, swinging, using a seesaw, and many others.

We went through each activity in the same order every day:

1. Riding a bicycle w/training wheels back and forth to a specific point, two times
2. Skating in-line back and forth to a specific point, two times
3. Hitting a ball with a hockey stick through a goal (3 feet away), one time
4. Throwing a ball back and forth, wearing the "gripping" mitt, three times
5. Throwing a baseball back and forth, wearing a baseball mitt, three times
6. Hitting a whiffleball off of a batting tee, three times

Going through these activities took 20-35 minutes. Because Brian only spent a short period of time on each, and they were done in a predictable order, the whole routine usually went well. He seemed to enjoy working on these skills.

Over long periods of time (months), I generally see progress, the main reason simply being practice. Brian seems to be able to learn almost any large or fine motor skill if he practices it enough (and he needs to practice it many times).

Large Motor Skills

> **B**rian had trouble learning to throw a ball. One day at a lake, he watched me toss stones into the water. I encouraged him to throw some stones and he did it without a problem. The very next day, he could throw a ball.

This is positive, because it means I don't have to think of special ideas or tricks for him to catch on. Simply doing it hand-over-hand, and then fading support, seems to work. He just needs enormous amounts of practice time.

For one activity—throwing a ball—he had a lot of trouble catching on. He just couldn't do it. After much work, he learned to hand me the ball, but this wasn't quite what I wanted. Then one day we were by a lake, I was tossing stones into the water and Brian was enjoying the ripples. So I encouraged him to try throwing some himself, and he did it without a problem. The very next day, he was able to throw a ball.

Throwing is not a problem for most autistic kids. In fact, many throw everything in sight. I once mentioned to a mother of a "thrower" that Brian seemed unable to throw anything. She replied, "That's a problem?"

After doing large motor skills for three years, Brian can now do the following: ride a bicycle without training wheels; slowly skate in-line by himself, without anyone holding his hand; throw a baseball and tennis ball overhand (he can't visually track to catch the ball, so I throw it directly into his mitt); hit a ball through a goal with a hockey stick; track and chase after the ball with the hockey stick (he can also do this a little on in-line skates); independently hit a ball off a batting tee (but can't yet hit a tossed ball).

Brian no longer needs activities to be in a predictable order, so we can work on these in any sequence. However, he can only tolerate working on most for a short period of time.

> *I'm pleased Brian is able to do these things now. While it took a lot of work and practice, it's rewarding to see him enjoy normal kid activities. He still has a long way to go, but when I see him doing these things, he doesn't seem to be quite so "different" from everyone else.*

Chapter Ten

Chapter Eleven

Computer Skills

Beginning to Use a Computer

There's a wealth of educational software available for children who are able to use a computer independently. Many families have their own. In addition, children use computers at school, or may have one provided at home by the school district. For those with regular access to a computer, I highly recommend the *Playskool Puzzles CD-ROM*. It's a gem of a program.

Previously, I bought a number of preschool CD-ROMs that Brian hadn't been able to use, because they required receptive language skills. But four months after acquiring the *Playskool Puzzles CD-ROM*, he was using the mouse to independently assemble jigsaw puzzles on the computer.

Initially, Brian wouldn't even look at the colorful graphics on the screen. Instead, he stared at the speakers and clicked the mouse incessantly. It didn't seem likely he would ever use a computer without support.

The "paint" program, called *Puzzle Maker*, changed all that. It has a vacuum cleaner function which cuts a wide white swath as it moves across the screen. It also makes an appropriately realistic sound.

In using it with Brian, I painted the screen a solid color, usually black, and clicked on the vacuum cleaner. I then had Brian hold the mouse with my hand on top of his. I held his right index finger down on the mouse—to prevent him from continuously clicking—and moved his hand back and forth so the cleaner "vacuumed" up the color. As we did this, he actually looked at the screen. This was the only software function that caught his interest enough for him to look at the screen.

After doing vacuum work hand-over-hand with him a few times, he started to independently hold his right index finger down on the mouse and move it back and forth. This was very exciting.

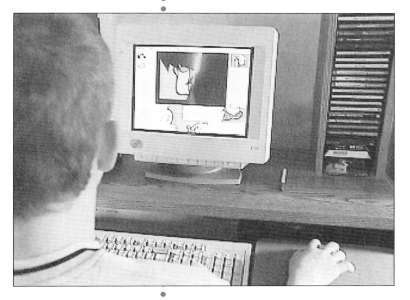

It amazes me how Brian can independently assemble complex jigsaw puzzles on the computer.

Computer Skills

Excellent Product Alert

Playskool Puzzles
This exceptional software program is available from:

Hasbro, Inc.
1027 Newport Ave.
Pawtucket, RI 02862
401-431-8697

Touch Games I and Touch Games II
Recently I've found some software designed for beginning computer users. Brian was able to use and enjoy these programs immediately. For information on them, call or write:

Health Science
418 Wall St.
Princeton, NJ 08540
800-841-8923

I then started to work with Brian on the Jigsaw game, helping him hand-over-hand to pick up puzzle pieces with the mouse and move them to the correct places. He'd look at the screen and was interested in what we were doing. Gradually, over the next three months, I faded my support, and he'd independently put together the various jigsaw puzzles. He even learned how to select new puzzles after completing the one he was working on. And he'd do the "Explore It" game independently, which involved moving complex shapes to their matching spaces on the screen. This game was similar to doing inset puzzles.

Yet, Brian wasn't able to independently put together actual jigsaw puzzles, nor was he good at doing inset puzzles with complex shapes. But he can do them on the computer by himself. And he's very independent; I can stand ten feet away from him.

After two years of working with Playskool Puzzles software, Brian is now able to independently do the "medium" level of the Puzzles and Explore It games and the "easy" level of the Dot to Dot game. He also understands and independently uses many functions in the paint program (Puzzle Maker) and he enjoys the Mix and Match game. In addition, he's beginning to work on two software programs that teach receptive labeling. Since he now has full control of the mouse and looks at the screen, I'm hopeful he will eventually be able to learn the nouns taught in these programs.

I want to stress that in order for Brian to learn the computer games, it was critical that he be prevented from repeatedly clicking the mouse. I did this by simply holding his right index finger either up or down on the mouse, as appropriate, and gradually fading my support.

Chapter Twelve

Sensory Work

I observed Brian's enjoyment of the various Sensory Integration (SI) programs he had at school, and wanted to try something similar at home. However, SI procedures require occupational therapy training plus large and expensive equipment, like rope swings, scooter boards, ball pools, etc. So I improvised and did the best I could with the materials at hand. I called my approach "Sensory Toleration," because it differed in many ways from a typical SI program. What it did was help Brian deal with specific intolerances to ordinary items or procedures.

The concept I used was simple: I had Brian alternately deal with "intolerable" and "fun" sensory situations. For example, he'd be exposed to an offensive, intolerable item/procedure for a short period of time, immediately followed by exposure to a pleasurable one.

I did about 5–10 intolerable items per session. A session usually lasted about 15–20 minutes and I did three a week.

We began with a one second toleration time for each item. For example, if Brian was learning to wear a baseball hat, I'd put it on him, count one and let him remove the hat. He wasn't allowed to remove the hat until I had finished counting. If he did, I'd put the hat back on him and we'd try again. When he'd successfully worn the hat for a second, he got lots of praise and was done for that session. I'd then let him have a fun item, like a spinning top, for a few minutes before the next session.

After several weeks, we increased the exposure to intolerable items to two seconds. Then after a few more weeks, it went to three, 5, 10, 15, 20, and 30 seconds. When he could tolerate an item for 30 seconds, he could usually handle it for several minutes or longer. At this point, I'd consider the item to be "tolerable" and we'd discontinue working on it, except as a review.

Some items became tolerable quickly, within a few weeks. However, most took a few months to reach tolerance and one took a year and a half (dental tooth polisher).

Sensory Work

The following are items or procedures Brian is now able to tolerate after doing this program for three years:

Items Tolerated
wearing hats, mittens, slippers, sandals, headphones, sunglasses, a baseball glove

Procedures Tolerated
haircuts with scissors, including scissors brushing against his skin; hair trimmer on the back of his neck and sideburns; toothpaste and tooth polishing

Here are some fun sensory items I used as rewards with Brian: (Note: they were reserved exclusively for the Sensory Toleration sessions.)

Tactile Rewards
toys with interesting textures
toys that could be stretched or squeezed
motorized toys that shook or vibrated
brushes (for rubbing hands and feet)

Visual Rewards
spinning tops
water drop toys
kaleidoscope

Kinesthetic
small exercise trampoline
small plastic indoor seesaw

Auditory Rewards
rain stick (a hollow piece of wood filled with seeds)

Initially, Brian was unable to appropriately use many of the fun sensory items. However, he seemed to enjoy learning how to use them, and over the course of many months, they were mastered along with the intolerable items.

• Some Details about Teaching Hair Cutting Toleration

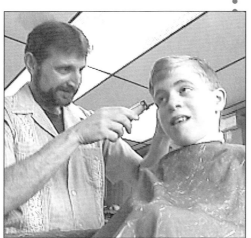

When Brian was young, haircuts were difficult. I would have to use all my strength to hold his head still as well as holding his arms and legs. As he grew bigger and stronger, I couldn't keep him still in a chair. Clearly, this was an area that needed some attention and we worked on it during our Sensory Toleration sessions.

When practicing haircuts, I had Brian sit in a small chair so his head would stick up above the back. And I'd snip with a scissors, about a foot or two from his head, to accustom him to the sound. I'd do this for a minute or so, and we'd be done with haircutting for the session. Gradually, over several months, I moved the scissors closer, until I was lifting his hair and snipping very near his head. I didn't actually cut his hair, however, because I'm not a barber. But, carefully I touched the skin

Chapter Twelve

on the back of his neck and next to his ears with the flat part of the scissors and pretended to snip there. It took many months for him to tolerate this process.

The hair trimmer, used on the back of his neck and sideburns, was another aspect of haircutting that made Brian flip out. I bought an inexpensive, battery-powered trimmer for about $20, and used it in our Sensory Toleration sessions. Again, at first I held it a foot or two away and gradually moved closer. It took him about six months to tolerate this. Today, I still bring this trimmer with us when we go for a haircut, because he might not tolerate a different brand.

But the bottom line is, when Brian gets a haircut these days, he's absolutely wonderful and cooperative.

• Whistles and Straws

During the Sensory Toleration sessions, I also worked with Brian on using whistles and straws. Although he was eight years old, he was unable to blow a whistle, nor could he use a straw. At each session, I'd show him how to blow into a whistle, and then I'd put one in his mouth for 10-20 seconds and hope he'd blow. There wasn't much more I could do, since hand-over-hand wasn't an option. I simply hoped someday he'd accidentally breathe through the whistle.

Finally, after eight months of trying this three times a week, it happened—he exhaled a faint puff of air. A week later, it happened again, so I realized he was starting to figure it out. Thereafter, each time I gave him the whistle, I wouldn't let him finish until I heard him blow it once. At first, it took a couple of minutes. Within another two weeks, his barely audible puff became a loud toot, as he finally got it.

Once he could blow into a whistle, we started working on straw use. At first, he blew bubbles through the straw and had fun with it, as all kids do. Occasionally, by accident, he would suck in and get some drink by surprise. But most of the time he just blew bubbles. Finally, a suggestion by his occupational therapist, to buy a one-way straw—available from an OT catalog—helped him master straw use. The one-way straw has a valve at the bottom that doesn't let the liquid drain out. While it wasn't as much fun, I wanted to give it a try. He used the one-way straw once a session until he pulled liquid into it, which generally took 2-5 minutes. Once he'd done this, he was finished with straw use for the session. Within a month, Brian had mastered straw use and could use regular straws as well.

• Summary

Sensory Toleration was consistently the favorite subject in Brian's program and he was usually happy for the entire session. For some reason, he didn't seem to mind dealing with intolerable items. Possibly, this was because he was used to the routine and knew he would only have to deal with them for a short period of time. Today, in the fourth year of his program, we are no longer doing Sensory Toleration because Brian has learned to tolerate all of the difficult items and procedures.

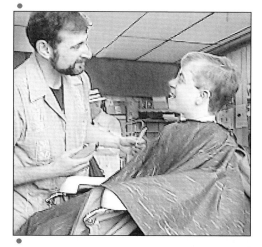

After months of growing to tolerate the scissors and trimmers I carefully used near his head, he is now cooperative when he gets a haircut.

Excellent Product Alert

One–Way Straw

The "One-Way Straw" is a popular occupational therapy training tool and can be found in many OT catalogs, including:

Sammons-Preston
P.O. Box 5071
Bolingbrook, IL
60440-5071
800-323-5547

Self-Help Skills

Chapter Thirteen

Self-Help Skills

Low Impact Toilet Training

I developed a non-intensive toilet training method for Brian that only requires a little time each day, one which parents can try when intensive approaches fail. It might also work for preschoolers just beginning to train, if parents want to introduce training slowly.

At the start of this program, Brian was eight and was bowel-trained. That had been accomplished over a two-year period by first sitting him on a potty, and later on the toilet, at the same time every day.

But we'd had no success with the other half of the toileting problem. Over a four-year period we tried many intensive toilet-training sessions, but nothing seemed to work. When he wore underwear, he'd wet every 10-15 minutes, while using the toilet to urinate only about every 15th time he needed to go. If he wore pull-ups, he simply wouldn't pee in the toilet at all, so attempts to bring him in every 30 minutes were always met with failure. In fact, the only reason I had him wear pull-ups was because he removed diapers right away. At least he tolerated wearing pull-ups.

One day, I decided this problem couldn't be put off any longer. However, I was working with Brian on many other skills and didn't want to drop these to spend a lot of time on toilet training. What I needed was a way to work on toileting in a limited fashion every day. I knew regardless of the approach I took, Brian could only use underwear, since every attempt at toileting in pull-ups was unsuccessful. I decided I could tolerate one accident a day, no more.

My solution was to put him in underwear for a half hour a day. I figured since he couldn't even stay dry for 15 minutes, there was no sense having him in underwear all day. If he wet during the half hour, he was put back in a pull-up and that was that. If he stayed dry for the whole half hour, he got praise, a sticker on his chart (choose any reward scheme you find appropriate) and he got to go back to wearing pull-ups.

I chose a time slot for this lesson that made the whole thing easy and workable, the last half hour before he went to bed, from 8–8:30 p.m. This way, if he wet before 8:30 I'd just put him in pajamas a little early, and we wouldn't have to go through an extra set of clothes.

One day I decided this problem couldn't be put off any longer. But I was working with Brian on many other skills and didn't want to drop these to spend a lot of time on toilet training. What I needed was a way to work on toileting in a limited fashion every day.

Self-Help Skills

His beginning schedule looked like this:

8:00 p.m.   Bring to toilet and change into underwear

8:30 p.m.   Bring to toilet and change back to pull-ups and pajamas—give praise and reward (sticker), if dry/unsoiled

When Brian stayed dry the entire half hour for three days in a row, I increased the amount of time in underwear by a half hour:

7:30 p.m.   Bring to toilet and change into underwear

8:00 p.m.   Bring to toilet—give praise, if dry/unsoiled

8:30 p.m.   Bring to toilet and change back to pull-ups and pajamas—give praise and reward (sticker), if dry/unsoiled

When he was dry the entire period (now one hour) for three days in a row, I increased the time in underwear by another half hour, up to one and a half hours.

When Brian was consistently dry for up to two hours at home during the evening, I asked his teachers if they could start putting him in underwear for the first half hour of his school day (9–9:30 a.m.) and start using the same method.

Throughout this part of the training, if Brian wet even once while in underwear, he was changed back to pull-ups for the rest of the day. It was a one strike and you're out policy and it worked.

When he consistently stayed dry for two hours at the beginning and end of the day, his teachers had him wear underwear all day to see what would happen. As it turned out, he was fine, and mostly stayed dry as long as he was brought to the toilet every half hour throughout the day.

At this point in the training (in underwear all day at school and at home), the rule was modified to "two strikes and you're out," because it was much harder to stay dry for an entire day than for just an hour or two. He was allowed one accident at school, but with the second was changed back to pull-ups for the rest of the school day. This required two extra sets of clothing to be sent in to school every day.

When he got back from school, I put him in underwear even if he had wet twice at school, because home was like starting over. He was allowed one accident at home and with the second was put back in pull-ups for the rest of the day.

Gradually, as he improved at staying dry at school and home, we had him wear underwear during the bus rides to and from school and for outings. Eventually, he mastered all of this.

I want to stress that this was not a quick toilet training program. It took 6-8 months before Brian was dry three times in a row for a half hour. But it was manageable and didn't result in horrendous amounts of laundry. Despite the initial lack of results, I persisted simply because I couldn't think of anything else to try, and I had to do

> *Throughout training, if Brian wet even once while in underwear, he was changed back to pull-ups for the rest of the day. It was a one strike and you're out policy and it worked.*

Self-Help Skills

something to solve the problem. It took about a year and a half for Brian to become trained using this method—*i.e.,* consistently staying dry all day, not needing to be brought in every half hour, and independently starting to go to the bathroom.

It should be noted, however, that Brian didn't always make forward progress. He had several regressions, when first starting out, and when he did I had to move him back to a half hour, because he was wetting too much. And he had one lengthy regression. After being dry at home and school for almost three months, he stopped using the toilet completely for the next three months. It was very discouraging. Eventually, I went back to the starting point (a half hour a day before bedtime) and within a few weeks he suddenly regained the skills.

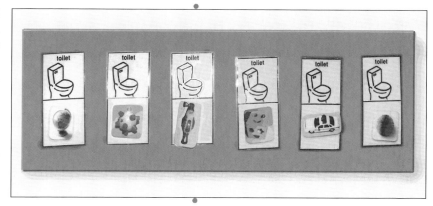

Figure 52 Bathroom pictures for night training on his bedroom door.

We're now working on night training, but haven't figured it out yet. Two things that helped (but didn't cure) were: taking him in to the bathroom between 10:30 and 11:00 p.m., and triple-sheeting the bed. I put a waterproof pad under each bottom sheet, so if he wets during the night, I only have to strip off a layer and don't have to search for sheets to remake the bed in the middle of the night.

The following idea (from his program consultant) seems to help him get to the bathroom more independently at night. I attached several picture symbols of a toilet on his bedroom door at night, and put a matching one on the wall of the bathroom. When he needs to get up to go to the bathroom, he takes a picture from his door and brings it to the bathroom, where he places it below its match. Carrying the picture with him seems to help him get to the bathroom. At times, when he seems unable to get out of bed to go to the toilet, I place a picture in his hand and he immediately jumps up and runs to the bathroom.

I've attached a photo of a special toy to the bottom of each of the toilet pictures on his bedroom door, so when he brings a toilet picture to the bathroom, he also carries a toy photo. In the morning, he gets to play with all of the toys that were on the toilet pictures he successfully carried into the bathroom during the night (see Figures 52–54).

During the day, I remove the toilet/special toy pictures from his door and bathroom wall because he's independent with daytime toileting.

(Note: most children will need to have picture matching skills for the "carrying toilet picture" concept to be meaningful. To grasp the "special toy photo" method, the child will probably need to have object to photo matching skills.)

Recently, I added a few more picture symbols to help Brian become independent with closing the bathroom door and washing his hands after using the toilet. He can do both skills independently, but requires a verbal prompt to begin either one. When I'm not around, neither action is performed.

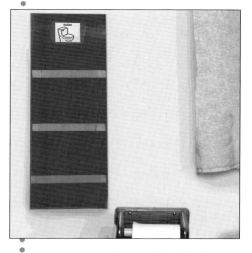

Figure 53 The matching bathroom picture in the bathroom.

Chapter Thirteen

Controlling Negative Behaviors

I put a "close door" picture symbol on the bathroom door frame. When Brian enters the bathroom, he takes this symbol from the door and attaches it below a matching picture on the back of the door. While attaching the symbol, Brian closes the door himself.

I put a second symbol, "wash hands," on the toilet next to the flushing lever. After he flushes, he picks up this symbol and attaches it to the matching "wash hands" one above the sink. While at the sink, Brian washes his hands himself. It didn't take long for him to figure out how to use these pictures.

This idea of using pictures to help a child move independently from one place to another (by handing him a picture and having him locate its match) comes from the TEACCH program. *(Note: this is just one of many ways that pictures or photos can be used in the bathroom.)*

Figure 54 *Here, Brian brought in one of the pictures.*

Chapter Fourteen

Controlling Negative Behaviors

Minimizing Aggression

Brian's aggression is of a demand-related nature, so during work situations there's more of a likelihood of aggression than free time. When he's left alone, he tends to be happy and to leave others alone.

Three of the ideas previously mentioned *(see Chapter One, Beginning to Work with an Aggressive, Low-Functioning Child)* were helpful with reducing Brian's high level of aggression during work:

1. to make it clear when he was done with a skill after completing it once (as opposed to performing it over and over again an unknown number of times),
2. to work on a wide variety of skills rather than one or two (which Brian seemed to like),
3. to never let him get out of doing a skill just because he was being aggressive.

Chapter Three, *Expanding the Program*, mentioned a number of strategies that helped Brian know exactly how many repetitions of a task would be expected. This helped to limit aggression during times when he'd be performing a task more than once.

Later chapters described new ways to break down the teaching of some skills. Presenting work at a level where Brian experienced success instead of frustration helped limit aggression.

Being able to express needs and wants with a photo communication system further reduced Brian's level of aggression, and using a photo schedule, which listed the day's work, helped him deal with transitions.

I want to describe one more strategy that has been especially effective at reducing aggression during work. I do it when I use the TEACCH pegboard to show Brian how many repetitions of an activity he must complete. When he becomes aggressive during a work task, I pull out all the pegs he's earned and tell him he must start again and do the work without pinching (or whatever he was doing). Likewise, if

Controlling Negative Behaviors

Brian's portable work schedule. This is a modified TEACCH work schedule. I've added a reward that Brian can earn if he completes all of the activities without aggression. I've also added photos of sensory activities (seen at bottom right of photo).

he's sorting a number of items and becomes aggressive, I dump all items he's sorted and tell him to start again. I will take either of these measures as many times as necessary until Brian completes the task without aggression. Being consistent with this strategy usually results in the aggression going away in a few days, since the last thing Brian wants is to have to do work over again.

(Note: this strategy won't work if there's no clear ending for a task. It's meaningless to inform a child that he must "do the task over" when there's no indication of when the task will end.)

While Brian's aggression often vanishes for several months at a time these days, it always crops back up again. Usually it will go away again just by being consistent with the strategies I have described. However, I often have to come up with new ideas.

The following strategy is one I used about a year ago to help Brian get through his aggression at that time. Currently, I no longer use the sensory items or the "relax your hands" card mentioned in this section. Generally, I use the pegboard idea, described above, and a few ideas mentioned in the next section: the portable work schedule (to show him activities he's to do); the special reward (which he gets when he does activities without aggression); and letting him choose items from his wallet notebook when nothing else seems to be working (he still has to complete the activity later). I'm also introducing a picture symbol in his wallet notebook to represent the concept that "this work is too difficult." These strategies are sufficient at present to keep his aggression at a minimum.

• *One Strategy for Dealing with Brian's Aggression*

This is the procedure I use for dealing with aggression during work time, when most of it occurs. First, it's important to set up a number of items before work begins. Brian's portable work schedule, which he carries with him to all work activities, has photos of several sensory activities he finds calming. Specifically, these activities calm his hands. I always keep these sensory items in the area where he does his work.

In addition, at the bottom of all task photos on the portable schedule board is a photo of a special reward. Brian gets it when he completes all his tasks without aggression. I always keep these sensory items in the area where he does his work.

When Brian starts to get upset during work, but has yet to become aggressive, I direct him to the photos of the sensory activities so he can choose one to give to me. Then I do the activity with him for a minute or two until he's calm and we can continue where we left off. On the other hand, if he doesn't calm down, it probably means something more serious is wrong, and I then prompt him to choose a photo from his wallet of an item that expresses his need.

Controlling Negative Behaviors

Since these items aren't necessarily nearby, we have to go get whatever it is he's asking for. When we resolve the problem, we return to work. Even if it's inconvenient to leave our work area, it's the best thing to do, because he's miserable if he's hungry or thirsty or has some other need.

When Brian becomes aggressive while we're working, I take out my "relax your hands" card and show it to him. He then must take his matching card from his wallet and give it to me. This distracts his hands, briefly, while I talk quietly and soothingly and try to get him to place his hands flat on the desk or on his thighs to relax them completely. After he's done this for a few moments, I prompt him to pick one of the sensory photos so we can do an activity, which hopefully, will calm him further. Then we can continue our work. However, if Brian becomes aggressive while we're working, when we return to work, we start the task again from the beginning. Sometimes we need to start it over several times, but he has to complete the entire task without aggression. In addition, if there's any aggression, he won't get the reward shown on the photo schedule.

If Brian is starting to get upset during a non-work situation, but has yet to get aggressive, then I just prompt him to choose a photo from his wallet notebook.

If Brian becomes aggressive during a non-work situation, then I take out my "relax your hands" card from my pocket and show it to him. He then has to take out his matching card and give it to me. Then I try to get him to place his hands flat on his thighs and relax them completely. Since I probably don't have the sensory items with me, I simulate the sensory activity by having him rub his hands together in the same motion as if he were brushing (*i.e.,* right hand rubs the left, then left rubs the right). When he's relaxed, I prompt him to choose a photo from his wallet to resolve the situation.

> *When Brian starts to get upset during work, but has yet to become aggressive, I direct him to the photos of the sensory activities so he can choose one to give to me. Then I do the activity with him for a minute or two until he's calm and we can continue where we left off.*

Brian and his family enjoy a quiet meal after Brian has set the table.

Chapter Fourteen 113

Summary

All the therapy ideas presented in this book have worked well for Brian. However, there will still be many kids who can't learn these skills even with these simplified methods. However, it's my hope that the ideas here will serve as an inspiration for others to find new ways to break down the various skills so the children they're working with can be successful with learning. If there's one thing I've learned in my work with Brian, it's that there's almost no end to how far you can break a skill down. There's always a simpler, more manageable, and ultimately more teachable variant.

While writing this book, I gave out a few chapters to therapists working with children who were previously unable to learn skills mentioned here. They tried out some of my ideas. I was pleased to see some worked very well.

For example, three children who had been unable to learn picture matching, were able to learn this skill using the method described in this book. One child, however, was unable to acquire it.

Two other children had the picture matching skill, but were having a hard time learning object to picture matching. Following the method described in Chapter Five, *Object to Photo (Picture) Matching*, one youngster mastered it in three days, and the other learned it in only one session!

These are anecdotal successes, of course, but they show promise that the ideas I've used with Brian have application for other children as well. I hope they will be helpful for your child or for the children you teach.

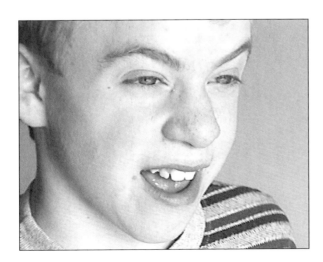

References

Thanks to Hasbro, Inc. and John Wiley & Sons, Inc., for permission to reference their products in this publication.

Excellent Product Alert

Special thanks to Frank Schaffer Publications for allowing us to reference their materials. Their excellent products are available through their catalog. To receive it, call:

800-421-5565

References

[1] Maurice, C., Green, G. & Luce, S. C. (1996). *Behavioral Intervention for Young Children with Autism - A Manual for Parents and Professionals.* Austin, TX: PRO-ED.

[2] Miller, A., & Miller, E. E. (1989). *From Ritual to Repertoire*. USA: John Wiley & Sons, Inc.

[3] *Ibid.*

[4] *Ibid.*

[5] *Ibid.*

[6] *Ibid.*

[7] Lovaas, I. (1981). *Teaching Developmentally Disabled Children - The ME Book.* Austin, TX: PRO-ED.

[8] Miller and Miller, *Ibid.*

[9] Frost, L. & Bondy, A. (1994). *PECS Training Manual*. NJ: Pyramid Educational Consultants.

[10] *Ibid.*

[11] *Ibid.*

[12] *Ibid.*

[13] *Ibid.*

[14] *Ibid.*